Critical Concepts™ Series . . .

Largemouth Bass Location

Finding Bass in Lakes, Reservoirs, Rivers & Ponds

D1522443

Critical Concepts™ Series . . .

Largemouth Bass Location

Finding Bass in Lakes, Reservoirs, Rivers & Ponds

Expert Advice from North America's
Foremost Authority on Freshwater Fishing

THE IN-FISHERMAN STAFF

In·Fisherman

Critical Concepts™ Series . . .
**Largemouth Bass Location—Finding Bass in Lakes, Ponds, Rivers, &
Reservoirs**

Publisher *Steve Hoffman*
Editor In Chief *Doug Stange*
Managing Editor *Dr. Rob Neumann*
Project Editor *Steve Quinn*
Editors *Matt Straw, Jeff Simpson*
Copy Editor *Kathy Callaway*
Layout *Amy Jackson*
Editorial Assistant *Claudette Kitzman*
Cover *Jim Pfaff*

Acknowledgments
Terry Battisti, photograph, p. 121
Mike Blair, photographs, pp. 95, 102
Kevin Brant, illustration, p. 80
Soc Clay, photographs, pp. 27, 45, 143
Eric Engebretson, photograph, p. 64
Alan Heft, "Tracking Winter Bass," p. 108
Merlyn Hilmoe, photographs, pp. 40, 79
Mark Krupa, photograph, p. 154
Bill Lindner, photograph, p. 16
Ralph Manns, "Temperature and Altitude Affect Oxygen Content," p. 77; "Weed
          Wars," pp. 80-81; "Habitat Separation of Black Bass Species," p. 82; photo-
          graph, p. 133; "Fish Watching," pp. 132-134
Gord Pyzer, photographs, pp. 31, 69, 112
Bill Rice, photograph, p. 146
Brett Richardson, photographs, pp. 92, 147
Hal Schramm, "Average Largemouth Bass Growth In Ponds," p. 98, concept of
          illustration, p. 99
Allan Tarvid, photographs, p. 33
Texas Parks & Wildlife Department, photograph p. 150
Joe Tomelleri, illustration, p. 99
Greg Vella, photograph, p. 8
Don Wirth, photographs, pp. 59, 62
Rich Zaleski, photograph, p. 105
Massimo Zanetti, photograph, p. 9

**Largemouth Bass Location—Finding Bass in Lakes, Ponds, Rivers, &
Reservoirs**

First Edition

Library of Congress Cataloging-in-Publication Data
ISBN: 1-892947-70-6

Dedication

To bass anglers, young and old, on the five continents that largemouths now call home, as you seek to solve the unending puzzle of finding fish. May this volume interest and inspire you in your search for the "zone." And don't forget to take those kids out fishing!

Contents

Foreword

North America has seen enormous changes in its climate, topography, and hydrology over the past 12,000 years, and one major change has been its distribution of native fish. Short of the changes wrought by glaciation, nothing has rivaled the changes humans have made to this continent in the past three centuries. We have farmed, built cities, railroads, and highways; dammed, diverted, and channeled rivers and streams. It's true that these engineering feats have increased overall fish numbers by providing large reservoirs with good warmwater habitat, and coldwater fisheries below those dams. Nonetheless, building on flood plains, river alteration, and damming have evaporated wetlands and introduced industrial and agricultural effluent to streams, making some formerly productive waters lifeless, as well as driving some species to local extinction.

This is where the hero of our book, *Micropterus salmoides*, the largemouth bass, comes in. The versatile largemouth thrives where plenty of other fish cannot. Today, largemouth bass can be found from British Columbia south to Brazil and South Africa. Stocking has introduced the species into Asia, particularly Japan, where many avid anglers target them. Largemouths thrive in parts of the Philippines, Central and South America, Africa, Hawaii, the Caribbean, and in several European countries.

Wherever waters warm into the mid-60°F range, largemouth bass can survive and reproduce. Where summer water temperatures range from 70°F to 90°F, water quality is adequate, and forage and cover satisfy its opportunistic requirements, largemouth bass not only survive, but thrive. These days, that includes most of North America's waters, thanks in large part to federal, state, and provincial water projects and eager stocking efforts.

The result is that in the last 150 years, the largemouth's distribution has increased from the eastern half of the United States—south and east of northern Minnesota and north of northeastern Mexico—to all of the continental U.S., five Canadian provinces, Mexico, and much of Central and South America.

In waters south of the most recent glaciation of 10,000 to 12,000 years ago, two distinct types diverged. Recent molecular genetic analysis suggests that the Florida bass is a species (*Micropterus floridanus*) distinct from the largemouth bass. The older type, the Florida largemouth, can't tolerate water colder than about 40°F. Largemouth bass gradually moved north as glaciers retreated, the melting glaciers leaving waterways of all sorts. Through natural selection, populations proceeding north developed tolerance for considerably colder waters. A natural intergrade zone apparently existed from what is now northern Florida/southern Georgia to South Carolina, where largemouths had a combination of characteristics of largemouth bass, formerly northern largemouth (*Micropterus salmoides salmoides*), and Florida bass. Where members of the two types have been mixed by stocking or through migration, crossbreeding readily occurs, yielding hybrid, or F_1, largemouths. Subsequent spawning with parental types or hybrids produces intergrade populations.

In warm climates, F_1 hybrid largemouths and fish from subsequent generations can grow huge. State record fish in Arizona, Arkansas, California, Mississippi, Texas, Louisiana, and Virginia have contained Florida genes. The current world-record largemouth—22 pounds, 4 ounces, was caught in an oxbow off the Ocmulgee River in Georgia in 1932, likely a natural intergrade fish. Lake Castaic in California yielded a 22.01-pound and a 21.75-pound intergrade bass in 1991.

In cooler northern waters, intergrade bass don't grow as large as their parents. More disturbingly, they can introduce the Florida bass' intolerance of cold water into northern populations. Other characteristics like disease resistance and spawning success can also be compromised. For that reason, responsible fishery biologists today resist anglers' urgings to introduce Florida or intergrade largemouth bass outside their present range. Since largemouths of different genetic backgrounds readily interbreed, introductions of non-native stocks can infuse maladaptive genes into the recipient populations. We'll have more to say about intergrade bass and largemouth subspecies in Chapter 2.

When it comes to other habitat demands, largemouth bass are well suited for the waters of North America's industrial age. Damming warms waters, yielding productive fisheries; runoff promotes weedgrowth and warming: these, too, suit the largemouth.

In-Fisherman's first bass volume in the Critical Concepts Series, *Largemouth Bass Fundamentals: Foundations for Sustained Fishing Success* (2002), provided an overview of the largemouth's physiology, seasonal and feeding patterns, habitat, weather-related behavior, telemetry-revealed habits, conservation efforts for these fish, and a bit about the world of bass tournaments.

This volume is more specialized. As a real-estate agent might say on another subject, this one is all about the importance of "location, location, and location." Our first stop, in Chapter 1, takes you into the global pond of the largemouth bass. In Chapter 2, you'll find an overview of their annual cycle. The next four chapters deal with largemouth location season by season, while Chapters 7 through 10 explain bass in reservoirs, natural lakes, ponds, and rivers. How these fish react to weather is covered in Chapter 11; in Chapter 12, you'll learn how to use new tools to fine-tune the process of locating your bass; and, finally, in Chapter 13 we'll take you on a tour of top spots for giant bass and learn current trends in producing lunker largemouths.

Introduction

From The Editors—
A Word About This Book

While you occasionally hear anglers say, "A bass is a bass anywhere you go," that's an oversimplification that can cost you fish, lots of them. Consider that the largemouth may well be the most adaptable fish species on the planet, existing—no, thriving—in an incredible array of waters on five continents. The species seems capable of gaining a foothold in new habitats and then evolving to maximize its opportunities to survive, grow, and breed there.

We know from recent genetic breakthroughs that the result, after many generations, is a suite of unique adaptations to environments. After a number of generations, populations differ in ways that may be hard to detect but should not be overlooked. The differentiation between the Florida and northern types (considered two separate species by some) is but the most extreme example of this process of differentiation.

In this volume, we offer a systematic approach to understanding first a bit about the habitat of the largemouth bass: From pits and ponds to vast natural lakes of the northland and sprawling impoundments at lower latitudes. Then we examine the behavioral variances, from general patterns to the most detailed data yet on bass location, gleaned from scientific tracking studies.

One key to locating bass is understanding the "year of the fish," from spring through summer, into fall, and then winter. We focus on seasonal movement and activity patterns related to feeding, spawning, and resting that will help you find fish all year. Armed with this information, you can approach waters anywhere with the confidence that you can solve any puzzles presented by the fishery at hand. Confidence can be an important aspect of successful fishing, and there's nothing like knowledge to boost this feeling.

The final piece of the puzzle is, of course, presentation—the choice of lures or livebaits to suit each situation, combined with the countless ways these baits can be directed toward our target, the largemouth bass. The next volume in this Critical Concepts Series will provide descriptions and solid suggestions about what works best in the many situations anglers face today. In the meantime, happy hunting!

The World of Largemouth Bass

**NATIVE
LARGEMOUTH
AND BEYOND**
_____

With the final retreat of the Pleistocene glaciers, largemouth bass spread northward from southeastern North America to establish populations near the headwaters of the Mississippi and the Great Lakes drainage, and east into New York and Pennsylvania. The native range of the species included the waters of the lower Great Lakes into southern Ontario and Quebec, the central part of the Mississippi River system south to the Gulf of Mexico, and north along the Atlantic coast to Virginia.

After the largemouth bass gained popularity with American anglers, stocking and immigration extended their range. In the years following the Civil War, a frenzy of stock transfers began. Between 1870 and 1894, largemouths were planted in almost every state they didn't naturally inhabit, and soon they were also stocked in five Canadian provinces. The building of railroads facilitated stocking. In *Book of the Black Bass*, Dr. James A. Henshall quotes a report from the *Baltimore American* (June 1874) that illustrates the zeal of early bass enthusiasts:

> "It was twenty years ago that Alban G. Stabler and J. P. Dukehart, together with Forsythe and Shriver, brought a small lot of Black Bass in the tender of a locomotive from Wheeling, West Virginia, and put them in the Potomac. From this small beginning, spring the noble race of fish which now swarm the river."

The first bass in Nebraska escaped into the Elkhorn River when a railroad car tumbled into the stream and liberated them. Establishment of hatcheries, or "fish culture stations," as they were known, provided fry and fingerlings for such stockings.

The two largemouth subspecies, *Micropterus salmoides floridanus* (Florida largemouth) and *Micropterus salmoides salmoides* (northern largemouth) interbreed freely when they occupy the same water, producing hybrid largemouths. Further spawning among hybrids or between hybrids and parent subspecies produces what are known as backcrosses or intergrades.

Florida bass originated in semi-tropical peninsular Florida and are intolerant of cold water. A large zone of natural intergradation between the two subspecies stretches from northern Florida into Mississippi and South Carolina. There, Florida bass as well as northern bass can survive. The dominant genotype is an intermediate between the two parental subspecies. This form seems to be the bass best suited for that region.

California was the first state to stock Florida bass. In 1959, several small reservoirs near San Diego were stocked with the Florida subspecies. The experiment was forgotten when results weren't immediate. Eventually, though, Californians began catching huge bass. The California record soared from 10 pounds to 15, then to 17. In 1974, Dave Zimmerlee caught a 20-pound 15-ounce bass from Lake Miramar, a Southern California reservoir. It suddenly seemed as if the new world record would come from California. In 1980, Ray Easley came close with his 21-pound 3-ounce catch from Lake Casitas, a reservoir near Los Angeles.

The response of bass anglers across the U.S. was immediate—they began urging their fishery management agencies to stock Florida bass in local waters. Stocking the Florida subspecies soon became one of the hottest topics among largemouth bass anglers and managers. The Texas Parks and Wildlife Department began stocking reservoirs with Florida bass, and the Texas state record went from 13 pounds 8 ounces, where it had remained for 40 years, to almost 18 pounds by 1986. Texas' annual catch of 13-pound-plus bass increased dramatically. In nearby Oklahoma, pressure to stock Florida bass became especially insistent. Anglers saw giant bass being taken from Lake Fork in Texas, less than 100 miles from the Oklahoma-Texas border, and wanted to get in on the action, too.

But the results have been less successful in Oklahoma than they were in Texas. The Sooner State began stocking Florida bass in 1972, and at least 70 reservoirs received Florida bass plants. Larger bass have been taken from Oklahoma's reservoirs, and three state records were set in the 1980s with Florida-strain bass; but nothing approaching the Texas records has appeared.

Climate accounts for a large part of these less-than-optimal results. The climate of Oklahoma is cooler than that of Texas, and Texas' is cooler than Florida's. Florida bass are out of sync in cooler environments—they may not spawn until too late in the season; they may not feed or grow well in colder water; and they can't withstand frigid conditions.

Other factors play a part, as well. Studies conducted by the Oklahoma Fisheries Research Lab show that the percentage of Florida bass genes in stocked populations declined steadily. This suggests that bass with Florida genes have not survived as well in Oklahoma's colder waters as have fish with northern subspecies genes. Natural selection is removing Florida genes: Such fish are less fit. This finding points to the possibility that even when the Florida subspecies is planted successfully, as it has been in Texas, it may represent a short-term gain with undesirable long-term consequences. Under less-than-optimal conditions, Florida-subspecies largemouth may compromise the subsequent vitality of their hybrid offspring and forthcoming generations of bass. This may be evidenced in poor spawns, reduced growth rates, or disease outbreaks in the bass population.

Unfortunately, anglers are less likely to acknowledge the cost of introductions and hybridization than to glorify the immediate gain (big fish!). It may take decades of study to sort the long-term effects of introducing Florida bass outside their native range, but many research studies indicate that native bass perform better than fish introduced from elsewhere. A Michigan largemouth not only survives and reproduces better in Michigan waters than an introduced Florida bass; it is likely to grow larger, too. Expecting Florida to thrive in northern waters is like expecting howler monkeys to thrive in Canada.

Largemouth Bass Distribution

Native largemouth bass

Present largemouth bass

Still, the mystique of Big Bass is so strong that some anglers want Florida bass stocked in their local waters no matter where those waters are, just to see how they'll do. "What's the harm?" they reason.

Planting Florida bass in an Ozark reservoir or an Ohio river is different from introducing a monkey into a Detroit park. The monkey wouldn't find a suitable mate and it wouldn't survive a Detroit winter. But a Florida bass might survive in an Ozark reservoir or an Ohio river long enough to introduce its genes into the local largemouth population. One careless stocking could mingle genes suited only to a tropical climate into a genetic heritage that took many centuries of natural selection to produce. Those centuries of natural selection saw millions of year-classes (fish hatched in the same year) of largemouth bass die because they were not optimally adapted to the conditions in their home waters. Those that do survive represent the best suited individuals for life in those waters. Wasteful and harsh as this natural regimen might seem, it produces fish superbly suited to their environment—and equally unsuited, in the long run, to other places.

After the largemouth bass gained popularity with American anglers, stocking and immigration extended their range.

Fishery managers now see the wisdom of conserving genes, whether subspecies-specific, strain-specific, or run-specific. They can do this by protecting local gene pools from contamination by fish that have evolved in other waters. Managers are looking more carefully at the fish they stock than they did or could in the 1970s and 1980s. Thanks to genetic sampling techniques like electrophoresis, DNA analysis and others, biologists can now measure genetic variations among subspecies, strains, and runs. This is one of the most important new directions in fishery management. In this brief overview, it isn't possible to address the particulars of genetic variation and adaptation, nor are they completely clear at this point, even to researchers. What is clear is that fishery managers need to err on the side of conservatism—"genetic conservation" is the term. When stocking is needed, it's better to stock bass adapted to local waters through generations of living there, than it is to stock fish from different habitats, no matter what their size. The wisest policy is not to tamper with natural selection.

THE INTERNATIONAL LARGEMOUTH

Having said this, what about all those places around the world where largemouths have been introduced? How well are the fish doing outside of their native waters? Where are they thriving, where merely surviving?

CANADA

When you think north, you probably think smallmouth bass; but tournament anglers visiting British Columbia, Ontario, and Quebec have been amazed at the quality and quantity of Canadian largemouths. Some of Ontario and Quebec's large interior lakes offer fine bass fishing, as do spots on the Great Lakes—Huron, Ontario, and Erie—and several of the provinces' major river systems. You'll find out more specifics when we go looking for giants in Chapter 13.

Remember that for bass near the northern extent of their range, the growing season starts later and ends earlier. Despite abbreviated growing and the open-water fishing season, Canadian bass can reach large sizes, primarily due to fast growth during the summer and long lifespans. And you can't beat the surroundings for beauty.

Mexican reservoirs attract anglers seeking fast action, big bass, great hospitality, and a break from northern winters.

MEXICO

Largemouth bass are native only to the extreme northeastern end of Mexico in the Rio Grande drainage, but they've been introduced to other parts of the country for over 100 years. Today, Mexico's hottest fisheries are on recently constructed reservoirs. Not surprisingly, Florida bass are the fish most often stocked; their preference for hot water matches conditions throughout most of Mexico. There they grow fast, up to the Mexican record of 19 pounds 10 ounces caught at Lake Baccarac.

Interest in Mexican bass fishing began in the 1960s, when Texans started heading to Lake Dominguez. Ron Speed, an early visitor, was so impressed by the fishing that he quit his job in Hemphill, Texas, to promote bass fishing on Lake Dominguez. Speed still promotes and books trips, but the hottest lakes have changed. Between commercial and sport fishing in those pre- catch-and-release days, bass fishing peaked and crashed on many formerly productive Mexican lakes such as Lake Guerrero, where the concept of the "100-bass day" was born.

Even today, Mexican bass populations tend to rise and fall more rapidly than they do on American waters. The problem doesn't seem to lie in water conditions, since reservoirs are deep, well-oxygenated, and offer plenty of cover and baitfish. Instead, it seems to be a question of fishery management—or lack of it. Commercial fishing is largely unregulated. Many fishermen use gillnets for tilapia and catfish with bass as a bycatch, and local anglers fish without regulations.

Moreover, most reservoirs were built to provide irrigation for large farms on Mexico's west coast. Dramatic water-level fluctuations have adversely affected bass populations by limiting spawning areas and reducing habitat during the warmest part of the year, sometimes resulting in fishkills. In short, the life of Mexican largemouths is often tough and short. They grow fast, but die young. We'll have more to say about the particulars of Mexican largemouth fishing in Chapter 13.

UNITED STATES

Alabama	16 lbs. 8 oz.	Thomas Burgin	Mountain View Lk.	1987
Arizona	16 lbs. 14 oz.	Dale Uden	Colorado R.	1996
Arkansas	16 lbs. 4 oz.	Aaron Madris	Lk. Mallard	1976
California	22.01 lbs.	Bob Crupi	Lk. Castaic	1991
Colorado	11 lbs. 6 oz.	Jarrett Edwards	Echo Canyon Res.	1997
Connecticut	12 lbs. 14 oz.	Frank Domurat	Mashapaug Lk.	1961
Delaware	10 lbs. 5 oz.	Tony Kaczmarczyk	Andrews Lk.	1980
Georgia	22 lbs. 4 oz.	George Perry	Montgomery Lk.	1932
Hawaii	9 lbs. 9.4 oz.	Richard Broyles	Waita Res.	1992
Idaho	10 lbs. 15 oz.	Mrs. M. W. Taylor	Anderson Lk.	Before 1962
Illinois	13 lbs. 1 oz.	Edward J. Waibel	Stone Quarry Lk.	1976
Indiana	14 lbs. 12 oz.	Jennifer Schultz	Harrison Co. Lk.	1991
Iowa	10 lbs. 14 oz.	Patricia Zaerr	Lk. Fisher	1984
Kansas	11 lbs. 12 oz.	Kenneth Bingham	farm pond	1977
Kentucky	13 lbs. 10.4 oz.	Dale Wilson	Woods Creek Lk.	1984
Louisiana	15.97 lbs.	Greg Wiggins	Caney Lk.	1994
Maine	11 lbs. 10 oz.	Robert Kamp	Moose Pond	1968
Maryland	11 lbs. 2 oz.	Rodney Cockrell	farm pond	1983
Massachusetts	15 lbs. 8 oz.	Walter Bolonis	Sampson's Pond	1975
Michigan	11.94 lbs. (tie)	William J. Maloney	Pine Island Lk.	1934
		Jack Rorex	Bamfield Dam	1959
Minnesota	8 lbs. 15 oz.	Mark Raveling	Auburn Lk.	2005
Mississippi	18.15 lbs.	Anthony Denny	Natchez State Park Lk.	1992
Missouri	13 lbs. 14 oz.	Marvin Bushong	Bull Shoals	1961
Montana	8.29 lbs.	Adam Nelson	Many Lakes	1999
Nebraska	10 lbs. 11 oz.	Paul Abegglen, Sr.	sandpit	1965
Nevada	12 lbs. 0 oz.	Michael Geary	Lk. Mead	1999
New Hampshire	10 lbs. 8 oz.	G. Builpitt	Lk. Patanipo	1967
New Jersey	10 lbs. 14 oz	Robert Eisele	Menantico Sand Wash Pond	1980
New Mexico	15 lbs. 13 oz.	Steve Estrada	Bill Evans Lk.	1995
New York	11 lbs. 4 oz.	John Higbie	Buckhorn Lk.	1987

CENTRAL AND SOUTH AMERICA

Largemouth bass have been planted in 14 countries in Central and South America. As in Mexico, largemouths have established self-sustaining populations in reservoirs and lakes in Guatemala, Honduras, Cuba, and Brazil. Honduran bass have reached 16 pounds, with bass over 11 pounds taken in Guatemala.

THE CARIBBEAN

Cuba reportedly has the best bass fishing in the Caribbean. When travel restrictions between the U.S. and Cuba were relaxed in the 1970s, anglers streamed to the island to get a crack at bass weighing over 10 pounds, and fish up to 15 have

North Carolina	15 lbs. 14 oz.	William H. Wofford	farm pond	1991
North Dakota	8 lbs. 7.5 oz.	Leon Rixen	Nelson Lk.	1983
Ohio	13.13 lbs.	Roy Landsberger	farm pond	1976
Oklahoma	14 lbs. 11.52 oz.	William Cross	Broken Bow Lk.	1999
Oregon	12 lbs. 1.6 oz.	Adam Hastings	Ballenger Pond	2002
Pennsylvania	11 lbs. 3 oz.	Donald Slade	Birch Run Res.	1983
Rhode Island	10 lbs. 6 oz.	Nicolas Finamore	Carbuncle Pond	1991
South Carolina	16 lbs. 2 oz. (tie)	Paul Flanagan	Lk. Marion	1949
		Mason Cummings	Aiken Co. Pond	1993
South Dakota	9 lbs. 3 oz.	Richard Viereck	Hudson Gravel Pit	1999
Tennessee	14 lbs. 8 oz.	Louge Barnctt	Sugar Creek	1954
Texas	18.18 lbs.	Barry St. Clair	Lk. Fork	1992
Utah	10 lbs. 2 oz.	Sam La Manna	Lk. Powell	1974
Vermont	10 lbs. 4 oz.	Tony Gale	Lk. Dunmore	1988
Virginia	16 lbs. 4 oz.	Richard Tate	Lk. Conner	1985
Washington	11.57 lbs.	Carl Pruitt	Banks Lk.	1977
West Virginia	12.28 lbs.	David Heeter	pond	1994
Wisconsin	11 lbs. 3 oz.	Robert Miklowski	Lk. Ripley	1940
Wyoming	7 lbs. 14 oz.	Dustin Shorma	Girl's School Pond	1992

CANADA

British Columbia	8.5 lbs.	Dean Ostrowercha	Vaseux Lk.	-------
Ontario	10.43 lbs.	Mario Crysanthou	Preston Lk.	1976
Manitoba	5.61 lbs.	Harry Ens	Lk. Minnewasta	1977

OTHER COUNTRIES

Japan	19.4 lbs.	Kazuya Shimada	Lk. Ikehara	2003
Mexico	19 lbs. 10 oz.	Bruce Newsome	Lk. Baccarac	1993
Zimbabwe	18 lbs. 4 oz.	Maxwell Mashandure	Lk. Manyame	2004
Spain	9 lbs 1 oz.	Guillermo Gomez	Ebro R.	2004

been reported. Puerto Rico also offers bass fishing in several reservoirs, though maximum size seems smaller than at other locations.

AFRICA

Largemouths have been stocked throughout Africa with mixed success. Stocking began in 1928, along with the largemouth's typical North American prey, the bluegill. Reports suggest that bass can be found in 10 African countries, with the best populations in impoundments in Kenya, Morocco, Zimbabwe, South Africa, and Swaziland. Stocking of Florida bass began in 1980 and they have thrived in the warm climate of southern Africa. Zimbabwe now holds the continental record of 18 pounds 4 ounces from Lake Manyame in 2004. Some populations are so healthy that they are holding their own in the face of commercial fishing. On productive waters, 4- to 5-pound bass are common, with 10-pounders not unusual. Bass clubs, including affiliates of the Bass Anglers Sportsman Society (B.A.S.S.), hold tournaments annually on the larger waters of Zimbabwe and South Africa.

ASIA AND OCEANIA

Thanks to their mild climate, the islands of Kauai, Oahu, Maui, and Hawaii host healthy populations of bass in reservoirs intended primarily for irrigating sugar cane and pineapples. Bass have also been stocked successfully in the Philippines.

In Japan, largemouth bass have become popular sportfish. They were first introduced in 1925 in Lake Ashineko and then to other waters as food fish. About 15 years ago, Florida bass were illegally imported and released. Their success has stimulated an avid class of affluent young anglers who support four major bass magazines and national tournaments. Recently, however, Japanese fishery authorities have targeted largemouth bass for elimination under the Invasive Alien Species Act.

Due to the small size and clarity of Japanese bass waters, bass have generally become more finicky than their North American cousins, prompting a shift to ultra-subtle presentations among Japanese bass anglers. Their tactics have been adopted stateside as top Japanese pros like Takahiro Omori, Shinichi Fukae, and Kotaro Kiriyama compete successfully in North American tournaments. Japanese tackle and techniques have made major inroads in North America, including the drop-shot rage. Japanese bass are usually smaller than North

Naoki Kohira and Jim Murata with a 26½-inch largemouth from Ikehara Dam.

American fish, though the trophy fishery at 7,000-acre Ikehara Dam produces many fish over 10 pounds. In the spring of 2003, Ikehara produced the Japanese record of 19.4 pounds.

EUROPE

Northern bass have been introduced into the cool waters of Germany and England, but apparently without success. Southern Europe is the bassin' capital of Europe. Once introduced into its natural lakes, reservoirs, farm ponds, rivers, and canals, the largemouth took hold here and thrived. Today, largemouths can be found throughout Spain, Italy, Portugal, and southern France.

Spain is considered the epicenter of bassdom in Europe. An international tournament that includes North American pros is held annually on Lake Caspé, a 60-mile-long impoundment of the Rio Ebro. Spain's fishery managers regulate the population, and it shows. Most tackle has been imported from the U.S., but the popularity of bass fishing is now spurring local tackle production in Spain and Italy.

In Italy, Portugal, and southern France, bass fishing is becoming organized, as well. Italy fronted the first European team to participate in the B.A.S.S. Federation Championship in 1998. Portugal has been trying to field its own team. Bass fishing in southern France is still informal, although the organization Black Bass France is promoting bass nationally.

In short, the largemouth bass has become an international star. In southern latitudes, the calendar periods we'll discuss in the next chapter differ by six months, but spring still means the same thing, even if it takes place in October (the Period for bass in the Southern Hemisphere), presenting new tactics and opportunities for anglers.

Italian champion Stefano Sammarchi with a fine bass.

Seasonal Aspects of Locating Bass

TIMING THE BITE

Largemouth bass behave rather similarly throughout their natural and introduced ranges. The timing and length of prespawn activities, winter movements, and other behaviors, however, vary significantly, depending on latitude and local factors.

In-Fisherman's 10 Calendar Periods accurately categorize bass behavior by season. Understanding the Calendar Periods will help you fish with consistent success in a variety of lakes, rivers, reservoirs, pits, and ponds. Calendar Periods involve more than water temperature: Often cues also prompt shifts in behavior and location. For example, bass crowd the shallows for a prespawning feed in response to day length, surface activity, and presence of prey, as much as they do to water temperature.

Some important concepts to remember:
- Bass respond to temperature trends more than to a particular degree on a thermometer.
- Temperatures can vary significantly from one part of a lake or reservoir to another.
- Bass respond individually to temperature and other environmental factors.
- Size plays a role in a fish's response to the environment.
- Calendar Periods are triggered by a variety of events.

Now let's look at an overview of the 10 Calendar Periods. We'll describe them in more detail in Chapters 3 through 6, when we examine spring, summer, fall, and winter locations. Here, we're going to focus instead on what the seasons mean to you when you're trying to locate bass. We'll start with spring.

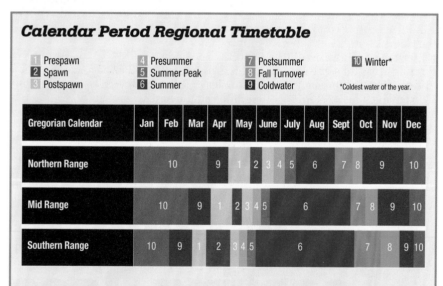

Calendar Period Regional Timetable

1 Prespawn	4 Presummer	7 Postsummer	10 Winter*
2 Spawn	5 Summer Peak	8 Fall Turnover	
3 Postspawn	6 Summer	9 Coldwater	*Coldest water of the year.

Gregorian Calendar	Jan	Feb	Mar	Apr	May	June	July	Aug	Sept	Oct	Nov	Dec
Northern Range	10	10	9	1	2 3 4 5		6		7 8	9		10
Mid Range	10	10	9	1	2 3 4 5		6		7 8	9		10
Southern Range	10	9	1	2	3 4 5		6			7	8	9 10

The 10 In-Fisherman Calendar Periods of fish response vary in length from year to year. Unusually warm or cool weather affects the length of the periods. They can vary as much as four weeks from one year to the next. The periods aren't based on the Gregorian calendar, so they don't occur on specific dates each year. Instead, the Calendar Periods are based on nature's clock.

In addition, Calendar Periods vary by regions of the country. The reservoirs of the South experience an extended Summer Period and a brief Winter Period. In contrast, waters along the U.S.-Canadian border have extended Coldwater and Winter Periods. Largemouth bass in Florida or Texas often are in the Spawn Period while those in northern Minnesota are still in the Winter Period.

COLDWATER PERIOD

Water temperature: Cold to rising
Fish mood: Inactive to neutral

This period occurs as early as late January in the South and as late as the end of April in the largemouth's most northerly reaches. During this period, water warms from the low 40°F into the 50°F range. Bass begin to move from deep winter lies toward shallower structures, where they resume feeding.

Bass in reservoirs typically move along creek channels or over deep flats, stopping in staging areas that offer steep vertical cover and feeding opportunities. When baitfish and cover are available, largemouths sometimes hold in large aggregations. During the Coldwater Period in reservoirs, they often suspend in 10 to 20 feet of water.

In natural lakes, largemouth tend to move shallower more quickly, because deep cover is sparse.

In the South, fishing can be good during the Coldwater Period, especially for big fish. Experienced anglers will note that favorite holding areas for some bass at this time of year are frequented for only a week or two. These are typically timbered holes in submerged creek channels, close to extensive flats or sloughs, often called staging areas.

With water temperatures still in the 40°F range, slow presentations tempt bass.

In northern lakes, the Coldwater Period in spring is short, with waters warming rapidly after ice-out. As they warm, bass move into the shallows over black-bottomed bays and canals. They're spooky in such waters, but they can be caught on tube jigs or unweighted soft plastic baits worked slowly. Several northern states and Canadian provinces close their waters to bass fishing during this season. This is an 'iffy' time of year weatherwise, so fishing is often inconsistent.

PRESPAWN PERIOD

Water temperature: Cool and rising
Fish mood: Positive

The Prespawn Period can be divided into three phases: Early Prespawn, during which water temperatures range between 48°F and about 52°F; mid-Prespawn, 53°F to 57°F; and late Prespawn, 58°F to 63°F.

During this period, dark-bottomed bays, particularly those along northwestern shores, warm up first, drawing panfish, minnows, and insects from the main lake. These, in turn, attract largemouths and other predators. Bass seek out the available cover, which at this time of year is fairly scanty (weed- and lily-pad stalks, stumps, and fallen trees). As prey species move into the warming coves, sloughs, and shallows, bass follow them into this clearer water. They see better here than in the upper reaches of reservoirs, which are muddied by snow runoff or by rain at this time of year. Water levels in reservoirs, natural lakes, and rivers are typically higher now than at any other season, so you can also look for bass in flooded areas—where brush, trees, and terrestrial plants, otherwise above the waterline, are now submerged.

Warming waters of the Prespawn Period may bring the best bite of the year.

Search out clearer shallow coves along the lower third of reservoirs: These often yield better catches than shoreline farther upstream, while the water temperature is in the 50°F range. Even in such protected waters, however, bass will retreat back to the first drop-off that offers good cover from wind or cold fronts. And they'll stay there until adverse conditions pass.

In southern reservoirs, bass typically maintain Prespawn Period behavior at higher temperatures than they do in the North, and they spawn at higher temperatures, too. Because southern bass spawn at a wider range of temperature, the Prespawn Period here lasts longer than it does in northern regions. When morning water temperatures on southern reservoirs exceed 60°F, the final phase of Prespawn Period has begun and spawning is imminent.

On northern lakes, bass become almost constantly active as the spawn approaches. This can occur at a lower temperature than in the South; as soon as the weak sun warms the water into the upper 40°F range, largemouths begin moving into black-bottomed bays and man-made canals. If you're blessed with warm, stable weather for a couple of days during this period, you may get fantastic fishing—particularly toward evening on sunny days. If you remember to move among lakes as their various temperatures rise into the low 60°F range, you can extend prespawn fishing in the North to more than a month.

Bass need to feed heavily during Prespawn Period to prepare for spawning, involving the maturing of eggs and sperm; so when you find them, particularly during the late Prespawn Period, they're aggressive and catchable.

SPAWN PERIOD

Water temperature: Moderately warm and rising
Fish mood: Neutral, but aggressive in defense of nests

A variety of factors affects the spawn. The most important are day length and water temperature. Bass can spawn at water temperatures as low as 55°F and as high as the low 80°F range, but most bass spawn right in the middle. Commonly, once water temperature rises into the low 60°F range, male bass shift from prespawn feeding to nest building. In northern waters, they'll begin spawning in the high 50°F range, while in the South, they may spawn in waters as warm as the low 80°F range. Not all bass in a body of water spawn at the same time, however. Temperatures in parts of a reservoir, lake, or river can differ dramatically.

In reservoirs, bass in the upper reaches generally spawn first because the coves and creek arms upstream usually warm faster, being darker and shallower. Spawning may last four to six weeks, with the largest bass generally spawning the earliest. For this reason, if you find a spawning area filled with small fish, chances are the spawn is almost finished.

Versatile largemouths can spawn just about anywhere there's enough water to cover them. They've been observed spawning in water from 6 inches up to 15 feet deep, though their nests are typically built in 1 to 4 feet of water. The murkier the water, the shallower they'll go.

But there's a tradeoff: Silt can smother and destroy fertilized eggs, and warm shallows attract predators eager to eat the eggs for their protein content. As a result, male bass need to balance several factors in finding successful nest sites. In reservoirs and natural lakes, they often choose channels, coves, bays, and spots along wind-protected shores. In rivers, they seek out quiet backwaters with medium to hard bottom.

Once they've found suitable nesting sites, male largemouths sweep away bottom debris and form rounded, silt-free nests atop firm bottom. In eutrophic, late-stage lakes, which commonly have soft bottom, bass may build their beds atop the roots of aquatic plants or build next to rocks, logs, or weedstalks. Such sites reduce the area they need to guard against egg thieves like sunfish, bullheads, perch, and shiners.

Finding a suitable mate comes next. After a male has swept out a nest, he seeks a larger female and nips, bumps, and chases her as overtures to spawning. Once the two are positioned over the nest, the female deposits 2,000 to 7,000 eggs, which the male immediately fertilizes. The female may spawn another batch of eggs in another male's nest hours or days later, which another male will fertilize.

After that, it's mostly up to the males, who fan and guard the nests for 2 to 5 days until the eggs hatch. During this time, males are typically aggressive in defending their eggs, and they'll often strike lures falling onto or near the nest. Their defensiveness appears to depend on several factors: Fishing pressure, weather conditions, number of eggs present, and developmental stage of the eggs.

Once the eggs have hatched, the hatchlings, sustained by their yolk sac, remain in the nest for up to a week. When they emerge as fry, they do so as a dark, aggregate ball, which the male guards as the tiny fish swim off to eat zooplankton.

As you might expect, despite the attentions of their father, not many fry survive. Spring conditions are erratic. Many fry perish when winds and currents push them into open water, where predators await; or water levels may strand them before they can seek deeper water. Optimal conditions include high, stable water levels and slowly rising temperatures.

Typical Spawning Months

AREA	MONTHS
Florida	January into April
Mississippi	March and April
Missouri	April
Pennsylvania	May
Minnesota/Ontario	mid-May to late June

The timing of the largemouth bass Spawn Period illustrates the region-by-region progression of Calendar Periods. Latitude, water temperature, weather trends, length of daylight, competition for habitat, and internal biorhythms are some of the factors influencing the exact timing of the spawn.

Not all bass spawn at the same time, even in the same body of water. While most adult bass in a lake may spawn during a couple weeks of ideal conditions, some spawn earlier, some later. Regionally, the onset of largemouth bass spawning may begin in February in the South and late June in Ontario.

This spawning pair of largemouth bass includes the larger female and male (nudging her side) in courtship.

During the Spawn Period, fishing ranges from poor to easy. Males are particularly vulnerable while they're guarding their nests or their fry; females are accessible because they appear in shallow water where presenting lures is easy. Females may also stay near nest sites, and they are vulnerable there to well-placed lures. Several northern states and provinces prohibit fishing for, or severely limit harvest of, bass during this period, because the spawn is compressed within a short period and the fish are so vulnerable.

POSTSPAWN PERIOD

Water temperature: *Rising through 70°F range*
Fish mood: *Inactive to neutral*

The Postspawn Period offers a short transition between spawning and summer's various feeding patterns. Largemouths take between three days and a week to recover from spawning; during that time, they don't actively feed.

Early Postspawn Period is solo time. Bass scatter, no longer adhering as a group. Female bass leave the shallow bedding areas they used for spawning and move toward summer habitat, lingering in deeper emerging lily pads and submerged weedbeds. Evidently exhausted by spawning, they aren't aggressive in striking lures or preying on smaller fish. For these reasons, fishing during the Postspawn Period can be challenging, but big fish are common.

To compound the difficulties, any one bass at this time of year may be in Prespawn, Spawn, Postspawn, or Presummer period in a single body of water. In reservoirs, they're likely to be holding near bottom until the water warms up and the weeds reach the surface. Late in the Postspawn Period, however, bass begin schooling up for the hunt. They can be located at this time by surface commotion when they terrorize a pod of baitfish, at which point they willingly chase a surface crankbait or topwater plug.

In northern natural lakes, largemouths are more predictable during the Postspawn Period. They can be found chiefly near boulders, wood, or mid-depth weed clumps and docks. Docks in particular provide excellent cover on natural lakes, where water levels don't fluctuate much. Backwater bays, where coontail, lily pads and fallen trees provide feeding zones, are productive spots for northern largemouths. Because water warms more slowly in northern glacial-scour lakes, these areas may hold bass for weeks.

PRESUMMER PERIOD

Water temperature: Warm and rising
Fish mood: Positive

With warming waters and longer days, weeds develop, and bass begin to move into the areas with the best available cover that harbors prey. Bass are typically aggressive at this point, as they need to feed to recover from spawning. A strong, shallow bite characterizes this period, a time frame which may linger if the weather remains cool and overcast, or may be over in a night if the weather turns sunny and hot.

In reservoirs, bass usually move to the mouths of small sloughs or hold in creek arms and shoreline points, particularly those near deeper channels containing stumps or timber. Now they also begin forays to prey on shad that are moving over main-lake flats. Other groups of big bass also move to offshore structures, feeding in 5 to 15 feet of water.

In natural lakes, large flats provide the preferred habitat at this time of year. At first, bass hover within weed clumps on such flats; later, when weeds sprout over deeper breaklines, they move deeper. Active bass feed on inside and outside edges of weedlines, or over the weeds.

SUMMER PEAK PERIOD

Water temperature: Warm and rising
Fish mood: Positive

The Summer Peak is short—the brief period when bass first move to their typical summer locations and the fishing is fine. Water lilies and other aquatic plants have developed, producing well-defined inside and outside weededges, but they haven't yet become covered with algae. Oxygen levels are high and the water's clear. Lakes are in the process of stratifying or have already done so.

Young baitfish provide plenty of food; adult prey have just spawned and are therefore vulnerable to largemouths. Unless early summer cold fronts become severe, bass feed aggressively at this time. In reservoirs with plentiful shad, some bass start to follow shad schools offshore, especially at dawn and dusk.

Locating largemouths during Summer Peak Period can be difficult. Some fish remain in heavy cover in shallow water, while others patrol deep weedlines, timber, and stumpfields,

Summer fun for all ages!

searching for prey. Shallower fish can turn off when wind or a cold front comes through. If preyfish are in deeper water, bass may remain there, often holding on steep vertical structures like points and sharp shoreline breaks. The moderate water temperatures and high oxygen levels at this time of year keep many largemouths in deeper water. Deeper-lying bass can be difficult to locate, but they're reliable biters because depth insulates them from minor weather changes. Locate them, and fishing can be terrific.

SUMMER PERIOD
Water temperature: Maximum
Fish mood: Variable

This is the time of year when water temperature reaches its maximum. Stratification has occurred on deeper lakes and reservoirs, and waters now become layered: A warm surface (the epilimnion), a lower level of rapidly declining temperature (the thermocline or metalimnion), and a deep, cool level (the hypolimnion) that often has too little oxygen to support bass. If the surface water warms into the mid-90°F range, sagging oxygen levels overnight make for dead fishing in the morning, or push fish into deeper water where they're harder to find.

In the surface zone, minnows, shad, sunfish, and other prey remain plentiful. Bass feed heavily but briefly, as they conserve energy by feeding when prey are most vulnerable—dawn and dusk. This can make fishing tough, since the bass are inclined to focus on particular prey and ignore everything else. Successful anglers try to imitate their chosen prey or attract them with novelty. This can be challenging, since dense weedgrowth demands weedless presentations and stout tackle.

Low oxygen levels in eutrophic lakes at this time of year can hurt fishing in early morning. Because of midday heat, bass usually hold in groups in suitable cover.

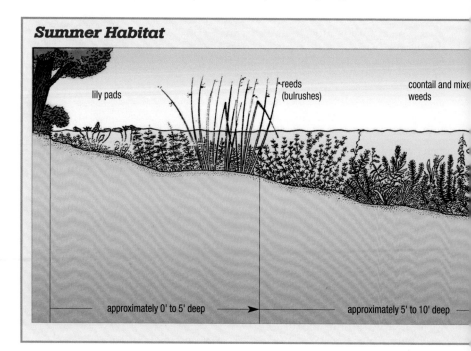

Summer Habitat

lily pads

reeds
(bulrushes)

coontail and mixe
weeds

approximately 0' to 5' deep

approximately 5' to 10' deep

Fishing at dusk or at night works best, now: This is when large bass leave heavy cover to prowl the flats for baitfish.

The Summer Period is one of the most stable and predictable in the largemouth's cycle. In the South, it's also the longest period—up to six months in Florida.

In the North, milder water temperatures and higher oxygen levels keep bass livelier and more consistently active during the Summer Period. Night feeding is common for bass in clear northern lakes and southern reservoirs, as well. Curiously, few anglers take advantage of this night bite, though tracking studies have shown that big bass feed almost exclusively after dark during this season in some systems.

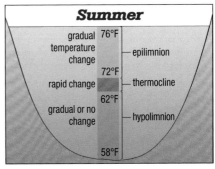

The upper (warmwater) layer may be from 12 to 40 feet thick, while the thermocline may be 2 to 15 feet thick. The lower (coldwater) level usually contains less dissolved oxygen than the upper layer.

POSTSUMMER PERIOD

Water temperature: Warm but cooling
Fish mood: Variable

All good things must end. In late summer, shorter days and cooler waters shift the largemouth's behavior yet again. In natural lakes, aquatic plants begin to die. Shallow lakes decline first; then, as water turns murkier because of wind and plankton blooms, deep weeds die, too. Bass that have held in shallow areas remain

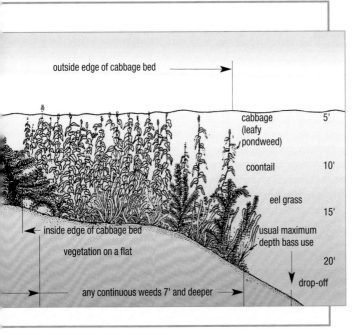

By Summer Peak, bass have settled into areas they use throughout summer. In lakes and many reservoirs, weedbeds become the focus of bass activity. Three general areas include heavy shallow weeds (slop); moderately deep weeds on the flat; and weeds along the deep weededge.

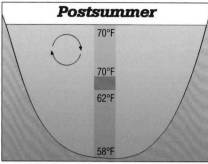

Postsummer

70°F

70°F

62°F

58°F

The surface of the water radiates heat to the atmosphere at night as water above the thermocline gradually cools. The thermocline remains intact but becomes closer in temperature to the layer above. Oxygen-poor water remains trapped below the thermocline.

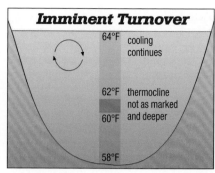

Imminent Turnover

64°F cooling continues

62°F thermocline not as marked
60°F and deeper

58°F

The thermocline shrinks as it approaches the same temperature as the uniform mass of water above.

near their declining cover, gradually receding offshore to the remaining clumps of green weeds in deep water—for example, along inside turns.

In reservoirs, bass behavior also shifts. When shad schools move toward shore, largemouth often follow them. Some enter creek areas as water temperatures drop, but they leave again when the water drops into the low 50°F range.

Gradually, as water temperatures drop, the largemouth's metabolism and appetite wane. Like the spring Postspawn Period, Postsummer is a brief transition between two seasons. Depending on weather and water temperature in a given body of water, fishing may be good or poor.

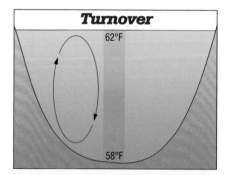

Turnover

62°F

58°F

The thermocline disintegrates, and water mixes from surface to bottom. The water continues to cool as it circulates, aided by wind. The oxygen level of the water drops for a short time as the oxygen-depleted hypolimnion mixes with the water above.

TURNOVER PERIOD

Water temperature: Upper- to low-50°F range

Fish mood: Inactive

As cold weather rolls in from the North, the surfaces of reservoirs and lakes cool, making their water heavy enough to sink and mix with cooler water in the thermocline below. Wind encourages the mixing, and eventually the thermocline narrows, then disappears. As cooled water from the surface sinks to the bottom, debris bubbles up to the surface, accompanied by hydrogen sulfide and other gases produced by disintegrating plants, releasing a musky or sulfurous smell.

Fishing gets difficult under such conditions, but fortunately, Turnover lasts only about a week on any one lake. Once the lake or reservoir has turned over, the fall Coldwater Period begins.

COLDWATER PERIOD

Water temperature: Cool, declining to cold

Fish mood: Moderately active to inactive

By the time Turnover is complete, a reservoir or lake's water temperature is usually in the 50°F range. Fish have abandoned their summer behavior and it's getting cold out there. This is when many anglers choose to end their bass fishing year.

But the Coldwater Period can yield the biggest bass you'll catch all year, so don't stow away your gear too quickly. Outstanding catches can be had when you locate groups of bass. Largemouths respond to changes in

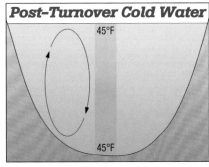

Post-Turnover Cold Water

45°F

45°F

Temperature becomes uniform. Wind action circulates and oxygenates water, which reaches a uniform temperature.

their habitat by aggregating around the remaining cover in their world. On natural lakes, green weed patches— coontail, pondweed, water lily and milfoil— survive until late in the season and can be found on steep, sloping structure. Before they move onto these slopes, bass that have spent summer buried in shallow weeds first move onto flats with weed clumps in 4 to 10 feet of water. As waters cool further into the mid-40°F range, they move onto or near drop-offs. Once bass move onto drop-offs, they can shift depth without having to move far laterally. Such areas become fall and winter sanctuaries for large populations of bass.

In reservoirs, bass aggregate in creek channels and along the outside edges of weedy flats. These locations make them readily accessible to anglers. If shad school deep offshore, bass stay deep, too.

As long as water temperature remains in the 50°F range, largemouths may continue to feed aggressively, chasing lures. Slow your presentations toward the end of this period: Cold-blooded fish slow down as the water cools. But you can catch bass until the day a lake freezes.

FROZEN-WATER OR WINTER PERIOD

Water temperature: Minimal temperature over extended time

Fish mood: Inactive

Even in Florida, there's a winter period—it's whenever the water turns its coldest. In southern states, water temperature ranges between 40°F and 55°F. In northern states where lakes freeze, water temperature ranges from about 32°F immediately below the ice, to 39°F near bottom.

Not surprisingly, bass at this time of year move to the deepest water they inhabit all year, because it's also the warmest. Just how deep, depends on the body of water.

In natural lakes, deep flats or basins of moderate depth, 15 to 30 feet deep, are common. In shallow, eutrophic lakes after vegetation dies back, oxygen levels fall, affecting all animal organisms. In some lakes, oxygen deprivation in deep water forces bass to move shallower. In the far North, winterkill occurs when water freezes deeply and oxygen becomes depleted. The largest fish, with their greater demand for oxygen, die first.

In deep reservoirs, bass may aggregate down to 50 feet or more, where they suspend in timber near deep creek channels. Even though they're inactive,

Largemouth bass are not generally sedentary in winter, and can be caught through the ice with finesse lures or livebait.

aggregations are so large that a few fish may strike a lure. Largemouth bass that are holding in water deeper than 30 feet may not survive the gas expansion in their air bladder, eyes, and other organs, which comes from being hauled out of deep water into our vastly lighter atmosphere. Largemouths are more sensitive to this change in atmospheric pressure than other members of the bass family. Plan on keeping any bass you retrieve from such depths, particularly fish that show signs of buoyancy, have the stomach pushed up into the mouth, have protruding eyes, or hemorrhaged tissues.

In shallow reservoirs or ponds, bass go as deep as they can go during winter. Sometimes this isn't deep enough; nearly the entire body of water may freeze or becomes so anoxic that fish can't survive.

In rivers that freeze, bass seek oxygenated backwaters and avoid current. Deteriorating conditions in midwinter sometimes prompt bass to move again. Good backwater habitat is relatively rare in many rivers, so large concentrations of bass can be found wherever it occurs. In rivers that don't freeze, bass also gather, and even at water temperatures below 40°F, good catches can be made.

Because of cold temperatures at this time of year, bass feed infrequently. They're most active early and late in the Frozen-water Period. Ice fishermen often catch largemouths through the ice, and lunkers are common just before ice-out. Tiny lures designed for crappies often work best.

Spring Locations

PRESPAWN THROUGH POSTSPAWN PERIODS I n the watery world as well as on land, location, location, location is key to success. And while finding spring largemouths within any body of water is limited to a relatively small range of possibilities, North America is immense enough that the very definition of spring changes by latitude and longitude. In April, for example, largemouths in central Texas and southern Georgia may have completed their spawn and headed into summer patterns, while in Oklahoma, Kansas, and Oregon, they're heading into their Prespawn Period. And in northern-tier states, every 100 miles farther north means a week's delay in the

In natural lakes, largemouth bass move into black-bottomed bays soon after ice-out. Soak a light jig and pork chunk near brushpiles, fallen trees, and lily-pad rhizomes for action from lethargic bass.

arrival of spring. In northern Minnesota, April commonly finds lakes substantially covered by ice, making the prespawn bite still a month away—open-water fishing can arrive as late as May 5th or beyond on some of the North Star state's big lakes.

In other words, when you set out to apply this chapter's advice on spring locations for largemouth bass, remember that while the patterns are predictable, their application varies with your own location. That goes for the duration of each pattern, too. A case in point: While the Prespawn Period may last for four months in Florida, it may be compressed to two weeks in Minnesota.

Of one thing you can be sure: As ice melts away in the North and waters warm throughout the largemouth's range, you can begin to spot your green prey in the shallows again. Hungry as they may be, the bass of early spring are no easy mark. Perhaps as a result of spending winter below ice or in deep holes, they spook more easily at this time of year than at any other.

Bass remain off-limits to anglers until their spawning period is over, in some states and provinces. In most of North America, however, early spring represents the first opportunity for fine, if sometimes challenging, bass fishing. The difficulties are common across the largemouth's range, and we'll review each of them here, along with the solutions that In-Fisherman has devised through 30-plus years of intensive bassing.

During this early spring period, some bass move into the shallows to feed, while others never do. Probably more bass can be found in black-bottomed mid-depth areas than in the shallows—particularly if you're looking for trophy-sized bass. Mid-depth fish are less spooky, bite more aggressively, and remain in one location longer than fish that move to skinny water.

But there's nothing hard and fast about prespawn bass, the reason this period of fishing is both exhilarating and difficult. Once you've detected a pattern, you may get some of the best fishing of the year; but if you can't figure it out, you may find yourself waiting impatiently for the more dependable summer bite. And yesterday's pattern may be futile tomorrow.

THE FIRST BASS OF SPRING—
PRESPAWN PERIOD

LOCATION

North—After months in a silent, ice-bound or coldwater world, largemouths are drawn on warm days to shallow, black-bottomed bays where the water is warm and the first weeds appear. Here, you can often spot your prey finning near the surface. You're unlikely to see them feeding, but after a week or two in the shallows, they plump up. Perhaps as a result of being in such shallow water, these bass shy away from the slightest noise or shadow. If your line and lure pass between them and the direction of the sun on the water, they're likely to disappear.

Northern bass that go shallow don't seek out cover or shade as they will a month later. Instead, they stay near the surface, because it's warmer there. Whether this is because the heat revs up their metabolism or brings on spawning, we don't know. Early-season bluegill and crappie often do the same thing. Bass in these shallows are ultra-spooky, and they're still lethargic after a winter in semi-hibernation. So, if you're following them, do it slowly and cautiously.

Canals are windfalls for early spring bass, because they warm fast if they're protected from wind and currents.

Although northern lakes may still be partially covered with ice—up to one third of the surface can still be ice-bound—the water temperature in black-bottomed bays can be in the mid-40°F to low-50°F range. This is plenty warm for bass to begin stirring and moving around. Because water temperature is so critical to the largemouth's activity level, carry a water-temperature gauge, or monitor your boat-mounted electronics while searching out these first bass of the season. Excellent fishing typically occurs once the water temperature has risen above 50°F.

It would be a mistake to assume that the only place bass can be found after ice-out is in the shallows, however. In dingy water, they often can be found at about 15 feet on natural lakes and about 20 feet in reservoirs. In some waters, bass hold in water 35 to 50 feet deep during winter, moving into the shallows when the water temperature rises into the low-40°F range. Although early spring is traditionally thought of as a period for fishing shallow, bass can be caught outside the shallows at 15 to 30 feet.

On developed lakes and reservoirs, canals have often been dredged to increase the amount of waterfront property or to access connected ponds. In either case, these canals are windfalls for early spring bass, because they warm fast if they're protected from wind and currents. Bass migrate into these canals as readily as they do into black-bottomed bays.

Bass often prefer dark-bottomed bays over light-colored ones in early spring, as they tend to warm faster and earlier. Even black-bottomed bays that lack adjacent areas of deeper water (3 feet or more) fail to draw many fish in early spring, however. Bass need deeper water nearby for shelter, when wind and chilly spring temperatures make the shallows too cold for them.

Central States—The Prespawn Period in the region bounded by Ohio on the east and Kansas/Oklahoma on the west (Oregon included, as its spring pattern resembles those of central states) begins in late March or April—earlier on farm ponds, and later on natural lakes and large impoundments like Lake of the Ozarks (MO) and Bull Shoals (AR), where largemouths wait until water temperatures reach about 60°F to spawn. At this time of year, night temperatures can still plummet, sending bass off their bedding areas and back to deeper water until a warm day reheats the shallows.

Ice-out Bass

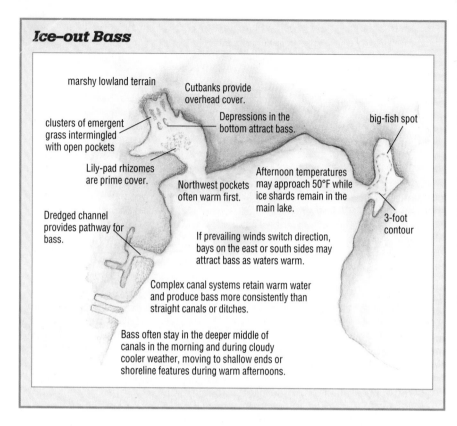

South—In the Deep South, recalls Editor Steve Quinn, largemouths don't typically enter shallow bays and canals until mid-February, when water temperatures reach the mid-50°F range. "Before that," he says, "bass stage in creek channels, holding in about 10 to 18 feet of water. The progression from winter patterns to shallow fishing is far more gradual than in northern waters." It might take bass several weeks to move from a creek channel to a nearby slough. Their position in southern waters is linked closely to that of their prey, primarily shad.

Don't think only shallow when you think early-spring bass in the South. Bigger bass in particular tend to be on the move, suspending in deeper water and moving into the shallows briefly, then moving back out to hold along steep drop-offs. In middle-aged (mesotrophic) lakes, which have deeper, clearer water and steeper drop-offs than eutrophic lakes, largemouths are more likely to be found during the Prespawn Period in deeper water (12 to 17 feet). Rockpiles far from shallow spawning grounds are the first place that lunker bass gravitate to in early spring on reservoirs in Florida, Mexico, Texas, and California.

Major Rivers—River basses' behavior differs from the patterns of their relatives in northern, central, and southern lakes and impoundments. According to John Pitlo of the Iowa Department of Natural Resources (DNR), who tracked the movement of largemouth bass and other species from their wintering to prespawn and spawning sites, bass migrate rapidly. They leave winter holes that contain enough oxygen, depth, and shelter from current at ice-out in March and April, heading directly into shallow bays that can't support life during the frozen period,

---

sometimes traveling many miles in a day or two. Pitlo's radio transmitters show that they move unerringly, too, knowing exactly where they want to go. Some transmitter-equipped bass have revisited the same spring spots year after year, bypassing good locations already occupied by other bass.

What do river bass look for? Their favorite spots are similar to those of lake and reservoir bass: Stump- and weed-filled, black-bottomed bays whose waters quickly rise to 50°F.

WIND DIRECTION AND WATER TEMPERATURE

Because water temperature is so volatile and variable in early spring, wind direction takes on greater importance than it does at any other time of year, in finding catchable bass. The old adage, "Fish the northwest corner of the lake," is mostly valid. Winds from a northwesterly direction are common in spring throughout the Midwest and as far south as Florida.

Why the northwest corner? Because the high banks typical of these shorelines block wind and prevent water from mixing in these protected areas. When the water has no chance to mix, the sun can heat it all day long, raising its temperature well above average. In northern natural lakes, canals in northwestern corners of lakes may have warmed to almost 50°F, while water temperature elsewhere on the lake is still 39°F and ice cakes still float about. Bass typically move into such protected areas about two weeks before they check out similar bays on the south side of lakes and reservoirs.

Of course, there's no reason to fixate on the northwest side of any body of water. What's critical in early spring is to choose bays on the side of the lake where the wind is coming from, since they're the most protected and usually the warmest. If the prevailing wind where you fish is from the southwest, then choose a protected area along the southwest shore. At this time, the sun's energy warms water, even if air temperatures remain chilly.

Here's the catch, though: Once you're in a protected bay, the windward side can be the best area if the wind is light. That's because the warmest water is the uppermost few inches, and the prevailing wind blows this to the opposite side of the bay. Wind piles warm water onto the windward shore, leaving the surface water cooler immediately offshore of the prevailing wind. But don't treat this as a hard-and-fast rule. If the wind dies down and you choose to do your early-spring bassin' in the early evening—usually the best time of day—the warmer water may be back in the lee of the prevailing wind. Your fishing will improve as you learn to read these variables, adjusting your tactics accordingly.

Early in spring, steep rocky banks may hold bass reluctant to move into the shallows. First search shallow sections, moving deeper if action is slow.

THE SHAPE OF A BAY CAN BE IMPORTANT

The ideal early-spring bay is not only black-bottomed but shaped to retain its water. If you've spotted a crescent-shaped bay with a broad mouth leading into the main lake, think about what that bay is like when wind pushes its warm surface water out into the main lake. It will be cold. If the prevailing wind pushes cold lake-water into that bay, it will chill down rapidly. (Bays that stay warm even when cold fronts arrive are those open on only one side or separated from the main lake by a narrow, winding channel.) Check maps of the lakes or reservoirs you're planning to fish to find such spots: They're prime in early spring because they're as insulated from temperature change as waters can be at this volatile time of year. This is especially important if you fish on cloudy days, because you have to depend on the warmth retained by the water from previous days' sunshine.

If you can find dark-bottomed canals, you're in luck. These have been dredged deep enough for boat traffic and are usually immune to the rapid changes that wind can wreak on shallow bays. Water here can be as much as 12 degrees warmer than in the open lake nearby.

During early Prespawn, standing timber calls for a vertical presentation that allows a jig to bump down through the limbs, always in contact with wood. Get as close as you can, considering water clarity, depth, and bass activity.

COVER

The biggest bass are wary when they leave their deep-water security. During the Prespawn Period, females tend to stay in deeper water, moving shallow to check the edges of spawning flats, while smaller males run up into the shallows more often. Both habitually use cover and structure. Even where woodcover has rotted away in older lakes, largemouths often continue to use those areas as if they still provided protection.

In the South, lily pads, rhizomes, and lotus stalks begin growing in February, so early-season anglers can watch for these. They're bass magnets. Bass are drawn to any cover—floating mats of dead grass from the previous summer, boat docks, stumps, stickups, beaver feed-piles.

In the North, with the warming of water in spring, chunks of mucky bottom rise to the surface, releasing swamp gas. The detritus floats on the surface, warming fast because of its dark and porous nature, and bass swim in and out of it in early spring. Watch for these areas—they're can't-miss spots for giant fish. Stump-fields and drowned timber also attract legions of bass.

Also check slight depressions in the bottom. These may be created when ice lifts pieces of bottom material or when stumps get pulled up or drift out of their sockets. On lakes, holes occur naturally. Depressions that are 8 to 10 feet deep attract bass. If they're a bit deeper, hold your boat a long cast away and prepare for some serious action. On a reservoir flat, a depression of only a few feet can constitute a migration stopover for bass.

Cutbanks are formed when a section of bog floats against solid shoreline, providing a canopy under which bass hide and also providing fine fishing. On mild, sunny days, bass will move to the edge or suspend near the surface of these cutbanks; but on cold, windy days they'll entrench themselves underneath, and you'll never catch them.

TIME OF DAY

Throughout the largemouth's range, afternoon- to early-evening fishing is best in the Prespawn Period, as that's when water temperatures are highest. For this reason, forget fishing at dawn, at night, or when there's a strong, cold wind blowing. Fishing on calm, sunny days is the ticket at this time of year.

THE NEXT BASS OF SPRING—SPAWN PERIOD

Spawning doesn't occur all at once. While some bass in a body of water are on their nests, others may still be in a prespawn disposition or already in postspawn. Because river backwaters, lakes, and reservoirs may be murky, it's often difficult even to tell if fish are on nests.

Many anglers forego fishing for shallow bass at this vulnerable and critical time in their life cycle. Others enjoy sight-fishing for bass, whether or not they drop a bait. Most largemouths spawn in shallow water, but 'shallow' can mean several different things, depending on the clarity of water and its substrate.

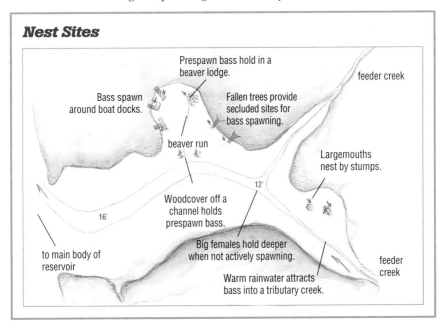

Nest Sites

Prespawn bass hold in a beaver lodge.

feeder creek

Bass spawn around boat docks.

Fallen trees provide secluded sites for bass spawning.

beaver run

Largemouths nest by stumps.

12'

Woodcover off a channel holds prespawn bass.

16'

Big females hold deeper when not actively spawning.

to main body of reservoir

Warm rainwater attracts bass into a tributary creek.

feeder creek

In murky waters, bass may spawn in water so shallow that their dorsal fins are visible; while in clear waters, their nests may be built in 8 feet of water. Nests may be within 40 feet of each other in prime pockets.

Once bass have released and fertilized eggs in their nests, the primary guarding duties fall to males—although females may hover nearby, as well, even holding in the scoured spot, at times. Males are at their most defensive as eggs mature and after their fry hatch; once the youngsters begin wandering from the nest to feed on their own, the fathers relax their vigilance.

Sight-fishing experts hoping to get rises out of males who are guarding nests or big females that remain on beds seek out the "sweet spot," the most zealously guarded area of the nest. This is frequently the part overhung by weeds or drowned timber—someplace where bluegills lurk, awaiting their chance to pick off eggs or fry. Baits dropped onto such spots are likely to get reactions from defensive males. These can range from close approaches to nose-down, pectoral-finning postures, which usually precede a strike.

Bass caught in deeper water at this time of year are likely to have completed the spawn and entered their postspawn, avidly feeding phase. More about this later.

LOCATION

North—In several Northern states and provinces, spawning bass are protected from angling. In others, only catch-and-release fishing is legal. Fish usually are found near spots where you located them during the Prespawn Period. Males sweep off silt to expose sandy or other hard bottom. They often choose spots with a log or stick on one side, perhaps because it provides a block against invading egg-eaters. Nest depth typically ranges from 1 to 4 feet.

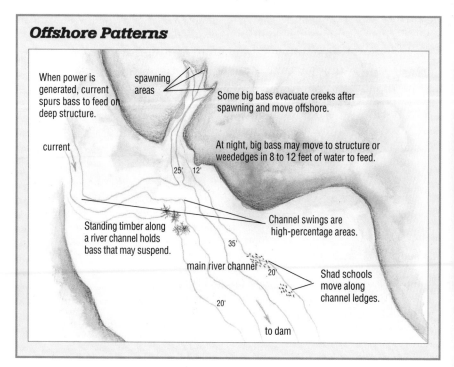

Offshore Patterns

When power is generated, current spurs bass to feed on deep structure.

spawning areas

Some big bass evacuate creeks after spawning and move offshore.

current

At night, big bass may move to structure or weededges in 8 to 12 feet of water to feed.

25'   12'

Standing timber along a river channel holds bass that may suspend.

Channel swings are high-percentage areas.

35'

main river channel   20'

20'

Shad schools move along channel ledges.

to dam

Central States—Bass in this region usually enjoy more predictable weather and a longer spawning period than bass in the northern tier of states. Spawning may occur over a six-week period in large reservoirs like Buggs Island (VA-NC) and Grand Lake (OK). On such impoundments, largemouths tend to spawn first in the shallower upstream sections, where the water is darker and warmer. The abundance of cover in such reaches enhances spawning opportunities there. Coves and bays nearer the dam face warm up more slowly, thanks to deeper and clearer water at the lower end of the reservoir, so look for largemouths in these locations later. Where shorelines on main reservoirs aren't buffeted by waves, largemouths may also spawn in the shallows.

South—In the South, bass spawn as early as December in South Florida, and they can be found in similar areas they moved to during the Prespawn Period. Because waters in the South are warmer year-round, bass often can be found spawning over deeper lake sections than in the

Big female bass hold near beds or swim among them when not spawning.

North. When you spot spawning activity in steeper, colder lake or reservoir sections, move on to check out structure on adjacent flats and drop-offs—you'll find active postspawn bass in those areas.

MAJOR RIVERS

Outside of the oxbows and sloughs adjoining them, large rivers offer bass few suitable spawning areas. The entrances to such spots can offer hot fishing for almost a month, while spawners come and go back into the main river.

If such shallow areas aren't present on rivers where you've caught largemouths before, you'll probably find spawners near the most protected shorelines or in boat harbors.

WIND DIRECTION AND WATER TEMPERATURE

Bass are triggered to begin spawning when water temperature reaches about 60°F to 62°F at dawn. As spring progresses, day- and night-time temperatures become more predictable and there's less of a difference between them. During the Spawn Period, bass spread out over a greater area of lakes and reservoirs as the water temperature rises toward 70°F.

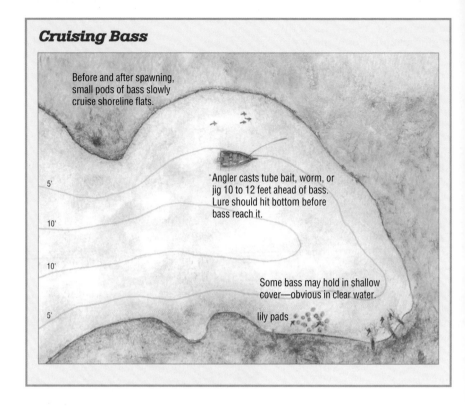

Cruising Bass

Before and after spawning, small pods of bass slowly cruise shoreline flats.

Angler casts tube bait, worm, or jig 10 to 12 feet ahead of bass. Lure should hit bottom before bass reach it.

Some bass may hold in shallow cover—obvious in clear water.

lily pads

5'

10'

10'

5'

BAY SHAPE

Just as in early spring, the ideal spawning bay has substantial shallow flats, cover, deeper refuges, and is protected from strong winds. The difference at this time of year is that with more constant warmth, bass move into deeper water. Besides looking for bass on the northwestern sides of lakes and in the most sheltered of bays, check deeper reaches of bays and the holes adjoining the mouths of rivers and creeks. Anywhere adjacent to warm, shallow water is likely to hold spawning or immediately postspawning bass.

COVER

In the South, lily pads, pennywort, and other water-weeds reach the surface during the Spawn Period. These, along with stumpfields in deeper water, provide the combination of cover and warmth so attractive to largemouths.

As water mixes in spring winds, bottom waters are re-energized with oxygen. In the Spawn Period, some bass take advantage of deeper water on the warm side of lakes and reservoirs. Weedgrowth in the North is scanty until the Postspawn Period, so look for bass around structure like stumpfields, docks, and concrete cribs.

TIME OF DAY

As springtime temperatures stabilize and rise, fishing can be successful earlier in the day than during the Prespawn Period. Afternoons and evening are best, however, because they give the largemouth's metabolism time to rev up.

Postspawn Behavior

During the Postspawn Period, male bass guard fry.

Meanwhile, larger females move into thick cover outside spawning bays.

The earliest spawners also begin summertime feeding patterns.

Allan Tarvid

Bays within Bays

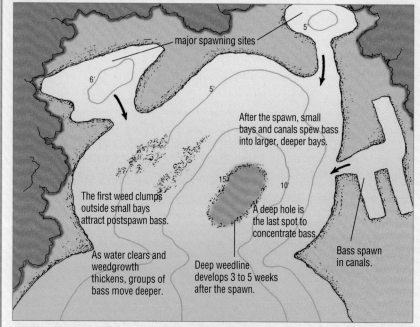

When bass leave shallow spawning bays, they often emerge into larger bays that slope gradually to depths of 15 feet or so. Fish from several small bays may gather to form massive groups that hold near weed clumps or wood but don't feed aggressively. Editor Steve Quinn's favorite presentations are a weightless Slug-Go and a light jig with pork rind or a plastic craw trailer. Large, lightly weighted worms also fall slowly to tempt these fish.

THE FINAL BASS OF SPRING— POSTSPAWN PERIOD

Postspawn bass often feed heavily. To do so, they have to cruise, as their prey are widely scattered. To increase your chance of encountering these mobile fish, long-time *In-Fisherman* researcher Rich Zaleski from Stevenson, Connecticut, suggests that you focus on two key Postspawn Period patterns.

1. ***Bass-Bluegill Role Reversal***—The first pattern Zaleski looks for is spawning bluegills or other sunfish. Once these preyfish start spawning, big bass begin raiding their nests. Spawning sunnies also lure shiners and crawfish and these, in turn, draw largemouths.
2. ***Opposite-side Preference***—Another pattern he suggests looking for is based on his observation that, while some bass are spawning on one side of a bay, bluegills will spawn on the opposite side. Postspawn largemouths migrate to that area, gunning for 'gills, and you can, too.

LOCATION

North—In the North, postspawn largemouths quickly resume feeding. Finding them depends on locating habitat adjacent to the areas they used for their nests. If there are flats and drop-offs near nesting locations, look for weed clumps on the flats and weededges, and clumps on the drop-offs. In reservoirs, the same pattern may develop, in addition to which bass may move into cover along the edges of creek channels, near the pockets they used for spawning.

Central States—Following the spawn, bass can often be seen swimming through the shallows. To sneak up on them, Missouri pro Guido Hibdon likes to sight-fish for postspawn bass wearing the same camo he uses for turkey hunting. Bass in the clear Ozark reservoirs he fishes are spooky enough, he feels, to merit such a disguise. "Cruising bass can be caught," he says, "but not easily. For some reason, they don't like a bait to fall in front of them, an approach that works great in deeper situations. They prefer to find it on their own." Try scouting for postspawn bass using the trolling motor, taking note of spots where you see fish. Return later, stopping short of the spot and casting to it.

South—In the South, a few largemouths may have finished spawning in January on Lake Okeechobee (FL), while others still may be guarding nests in April.

It's a large, variable region, with altitude and longitude playing as significant a role as latitude does in the North. Highland impoundments in the Southeast, for example, tend to be murkier than those of the Ozarks, and both are clearer than the hill-land reservoirs of the Plains states, which are roiled continuously by that region's heavy winds. Florida's natural lakes, on the other hand, have become unnaturally clear as the exotic weed hydrilla expands its range, filtering out nutrients and silt. Also, coastal regions are milder than interior ones due to the ocean's steadying influence on temperature. Expect earlier and more prolonged spawning cycles along the East and West coasts.

MAJOR RIVERS

In clear rivers, postspawn bass hold under trees or by stumps. Like trout in coldwater streams, they face into the current, finning to maintain their location. Pro Shaw Grigsby scouts and hunts them using tactics similar to those of fly fishermen: Light lines, delicate equipment, and drifts that resemble natural prey tumbling down a river's currents.

The spring calendar periods lure anglers to start the season right. There's potential for the biggest bass of the year.

WIND DIRECTION AND WATER TEMPERATURE

Wind direction and water temperature become less critical than they were in early spring, after postspawn largemouths move out into the main body of lakes and reservoirs.

BAY SHAPE

The ideal Postspawn Period bay offers access to the main lake or reservoir and holes adjoining the mouths of rivers and creeks. Deeper spots adjacent to warm, shallow water are likely to hold postspawn bass, particularly if they offer cover, structure, and baitfish. In reservoirs, look for major points in the middle and lower sections of creek arms, where cover and depth variation offer hiding and feeding opportunities.

COVER

Milfoil, hydrilla, and other types of vegetation provide postspawn bass with both food and cover, and their edges now provide anglers with the best location for encountering postspawn bass. Focus on the inside weededges: First, large-mouths use this narrow corridor to corner prey. Schools of shiners and small shad run these edges, and sunfish spawn on the sandy flats inside them. As weeds become thicker and taller, this outside edge becomes the major feeding location for large bass.

On large southern impoundments with little submerged vegetation, look for structure rather than natural cover—secondary points and creek and river channels near the edges of main river channels, in depths of 10 to 25 feet. Creek channels with depths in the 20-foot range hold bass if shad are abundant there; sometimes largemouths remain in such locations throughout the summer. Big females may also move to humps and deep ridges soon after spawning, offering outstanding lunker action in the early season.

In northern and central states, submergent and emergent aquatic vegetation blooms during the Postspawn Period, after which bass can be found in weedbeds as well as around structure.

TIME OF DAY

Once springtime air and water temperatures have risen and stabilized, fishing becomes successful early in the day. And don't discount night-fishing. In the South, postspawn bass feed after dark along breaklines in grassy lakes. This is when they're most vulnerable.

In the next chapter, we turn to the largemouth's summer locations, when the livin' is easy and the fishing ranges from easy to tough.

Summer Locations

PRESUMMER THROUGH POSTSUMMER PERIODS

Summertime, and the living is easy in the largemouth's world. As water warms and bass complete their spawn, they begin to spread out over larger areas, often near vegetation. From the Postspawn Period until Fall Turnover, many of the biggest bass in natural lakes and reservoirs live in the shade of coontail, angel hair, bladderwort, elephant ear, parrot feather, cattail, lily pads, hydrilla, milfoil, water hyacinth, or other aquatic plant species.

It's long been the faith of largemouth anglers that summer fish are caught shallow beneath such typically bassy cover as lily pads, reed and cane patches, fallen trees and stumps or boat docks, but this is hardly the entire story. In this chapter, we'll explore the wider range of summer bass locations.

BASS ON THE EDGE

Ecologists use the term 'edge effect' to describe the preference of land and water creatures for locations that offer them the advantages of both cover and range. Bass share this affinity for edges, or breaks, as they're often called. Particularly during the early part of the summer season, edges in the shallows are likely to hold the greatest number of bass.

Some edges, such as those formed by weedbeds, have two sides: an inside and an outside. During the first month of postspawn bass fishing, it's usually the inside edge that you want to concentrate on. Bass use the inside edges of emergent or mature weedgrowth to find and corner prey. Those are also the spots where they built their spawning beds earlier in the season, and they often linger here for weeks afterward.

Inside edges often aren't as obvious to the naked eye as the outside ones, for the simple reason that the latter signal where a steep drop-off or other change in structure begins. In contrast, inside edges are subtler and shallower. Locate them by motoring across surface vegetation until it thins near the shore. Many plant species don't thrive in water less than 3 or 4 feet deep, and you'll have to go in close to find the inside edge.

On northern lakes, ice over the shallows, when it swells and cracks, can literally pluck shallow vegetation from the bottom, so weeds can be slow to reestablish themselves in summer. On many reservoirs, inside weededges form during annual fall and winter drawdowns. When water rises again in spring, the weededge is well offshore. Fluctuations in water levels, particularly in drought years, may lay bare areas of fertile soil that sprout terrestrial grasses, shrubs, even small trees. When these areas flood after the impoundment refills, a new inside edge is formed by the now-flooded vegetation, attracting bass that can be fished throughout the Postspawn through Postsummer Periods.

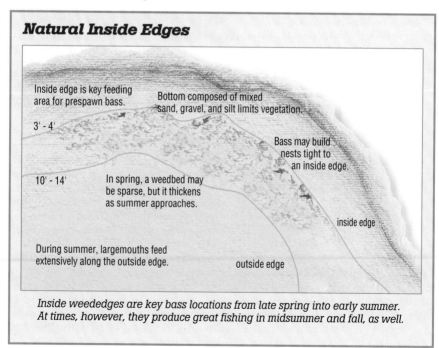

Natural Inside Edges

Inside edge is key feeding area for prespawn bass.

Bottom composed of mixed sand, gravel, and silt limits vegetation.

3' - 4'

Bass may build nests tight to an inside edge.

10' - 14'

In spring, a weedbed may be sparse, but it thickens as summer approaches.

inside edge

During summer, largemouths feed extensively along the outside edge.

outside edge

Inside weededges are key bass locations from late spring into early summer. At times, however, they produce great fishing in midsummer and fall, as well.

In most waters, inside edges lose some of their appeal once deeper weedlines develop. There are exceptions to this observation, however. Where distinct inside edges occur in the open water of natural lakes and reservoirs, groups of active bass run them early in the day in pursuit of bream, crayfish, and shiners. Afterwards, they may retire into dense weeds, holding along the outside weed-edge, or may move onto deeper structure. But their early flurry in the weed forest is often the hottest bite of the day.

In northern lakes with big pike and muskies, largemouth bass are less likely to abandon inside edges. Anglers speculate that these larger predators keep largemouths in their (inside) place by patrolling the outside of the weed-edges. Angling experience as well as underwater cameras confirm this pattern on some northern lakes: Largemouths make extensive use of shallow emergent vegetation, feeding along the inside edges of maidencane, bulrushes, wild rice, and lily pads.

In reservoirs, inside edges include submerged roadbeds and riprap banks. There, plants thin or stop where gravel or asphalt roadways or boulders interfere with their growth. The resulting edges are clearly visible, with rock or pavement on one side and a wall of vegetation on the other. Hot summer bites occur in such locations at dawn and dusk, as well as when wind and waves pound against them, dislodging baitfish and invertebrates.

Let's look more closely at what weedgrowth offers largemouths, as a prelude to thinking about what weededges and weedgrowth offer you.

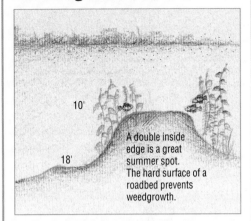

Submerged Roadbeds

10'

18'

A double inside edge is a great summer spot. The hard surface of a roadbed prevents weedgrowth.

In impoundments, manmade structures like roadbeads are great summer spots.

WITHIN THE WEEDS

The new generation of underwater cameras reveals views of weededges that can help you rethink basses' summer locations. Initially, when you approach weedbeds from open water, they look like the wall fronting the Emerald City of Oz: steep, solid, and glowing, as if lit from within. Closer up, however, the illusion of solidity disappears, replaced by a green latticework that's thickest at the water's surface and far more permeable down where plant stalks emerge from bottom.

Vegetation may look at first like a green wall, but it functions more like a curtain of hanging beads across a doorway. Bass swim easily through and under canopies of water weeds. Here, the light is dim and the vistas short. The whole place looks green and obscure. Bass in weeds don't have the opportunity to inspect very closely whatever prey come by, the reason they're often easy to get a rise from in weeds. If your bait or lure looks or sounds even slightly plausible, they may strike it.

Even in clear shallow water, largemouth bass feed among weedstalks all summer long.

Merlyn Hilmoe

As summer progresses, bass move deeper into the weeds. Groups and individuals swim along the outside of vegetation, stopping to inspect pockets, points, and anything else that may hold preyfish. They may also bury themselves within the weeds, holding on bottom or under the canopy. Weeds, in short, are locations always worth checking. But you've got to cover a lot of weededges to find what you're looking for.

BASS BOTANY 101

Weeds begin their seasonal growth when water warms into the upper 50°F range, with many species reaching their maximum growth in late summer. Once they break the surface and spread into mats, these become life rafts for insects, birds, and amphibians. Beneath them live golden shiners, bluegills, and other small fish that typically make up a bass's diet.

Bass patterns often revolve around particular plant species, so it pays to know your local varieties and how bass relate to them. Here are a few of the largemouth's favorite salad greens, and why:

Lily pads—In midsummer, the best fishing for aggressive largemouths usually occurs in lily pad fields, both yellow (spadderdock) and white (fragrant) species. Some lily roots, called rhizomes, are over 40 feet long, with hundreds of stalks. These are densest near bottom and spread toward the surface, providing room for bluegills to peck at worms and for bass to hunt. Bass usually hold directly beneath the pads; sometimes you can even see their dorsal fins and tails breaking the surface. If you're faced with a choice between a field of only lily pads and a mat of mixed vegetable, though, choose the latter—it's likely to yield more fish.

lily pads

Filamentous algae—These slimy forms of colonial algae grow in clumps and strands that float on the surface or in midwater, inflated by the gas they produce. They're usually found in quiet, warm bays in early summer. Big bass are crazy about this stuff. In small, fertile lakes, algae mats may persist all summer, drawing bass to its cover. In some lakes, however, water temperature in midsummer appears to kill it off. Algae, like duckweed, forms carpets so dense that bass may hold beneath them in only 2 to 3 feet of water.

Blue-green algae—Often blackish in color, it forms mats so dense that bass seem to know they can't blast through them. Thinner clumps sometimes hold fish in waters where more desirable vegetation is lacking.

Water hyacinth—This large, exotic floating species persists despite efforts by lake associations and other weed-control experts to kill it off. Boaters may not like it, but bass love it. Water hyacinths provide plenty of shade for bass, as well as for the many invertebrates that attract the largemouth's prey. If you spot water hyacinths, chances are that bass are lying somewhere beneath the canopy.

Duckweed—Midsummer brings heavy carpets of duckweed, a collection of small, roundish, single-leafed species. They typically colonize lakes and reservoirs with high inputs of nutrients from lawns, farm runoff, sewers, and other pollution. Duckweed multiplies quickly in warm water. If you find a patch or shoal of it near the mouth of a cove or along the edge of a river backwater, chances are you'll encounter a big bite when bass are present. Duckweed, however, because it's so light, shifts location with wind direction; so, when considering it as a possible bass location, you need to factor in not only the weed itself but what lies beneath it. If it's coating stumps, logs, and brush in 4 to 10 feet of water, you may enjoy some of the most dramatic bassin' you've ever had.

Eurasian milfoil—An exotic from Europe that has spread across North America from Florida to Ontario, milfoil is bad news for boaters and shorefront property owners, but good news for largemouths and those who hunt them. Vast milfoil beds have turned barren flats into bass havens throughout the South. Milfoil typically grows in 3 to 12 feet of water, the favorite summer depth-range for largemouths. Northern milfoil, a native species, also forms thick clumps, though it never reaches the density of the Eurasian species.

Hydrilla—This exotic is supplanting milfoil in some southern reservoirs, where it also clears the water. It can mat in 20 feet of water, making it tough to get a boat through. Sometimes hydrilla dies back from late-summer sun.

Cabbage—On natural lakes in the North, a prime Postspawn Period location is the transition area where backwater bays give way to boulders and broadleaf pondweed species often called cabbage. Such sites offer terrific feeding areas for largemouths, and the fish often remain in them into fall.

Coontail—This lush submerged plant is a late bloomer, increasing in coverage and density in midsummer and peaking in early fall. A bass magnet, wherever found.

Curlyleaf Pondweed—Another fast-growing exotic, this submergent species quickly colonizes shallow flats and bays in late spring. Intolerant of summer heat, it thins in early summer, often giving way to other species. While it can form thick clumps, bass use its edges and pockets for feeding zones.

milfoil

hydrilla

curlyleaf pondweed

coontail

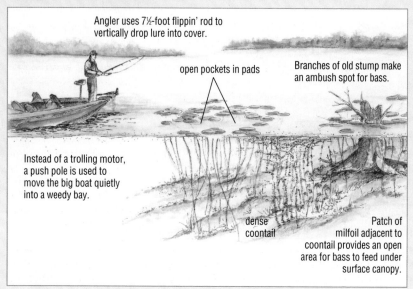

Flippin' the Pads

Angler uses 7½-foot flippin' rod to vertically drop lure into cover.

open pockets in pads

Branches of old stump make an ambush spot for bass.

Instead of a trolling motor, a push pole is used to move the big boat quietly into a weedy bay.

dense coontail

Patch of milfoil adjacent to coontail provides an open area for bass to feed under surface canopy.

Lily-pad bays, sometimes called "slop," hold huge bass all summer long. Careful presentations with heavy tackle are the key.

WEEDS AND WEATHER

Not surprisingly, weather interacts with the plants that bass use for cover. Knowing what to expect can help you determine when and where to fish.

In the Presummer Period, hot afternoon sunshine warms weedbeds and algae mats. Oxygen levels and pH rise dramatically, stimulating preyfish and bass. Cool nights reduce fish activity.

When duckweed, algae, and other weeds become thick, oxygen content drops significantly at night. On humid, overcast days with little wind, however, edges and pockets of weedbeds and lily pads yield intense bass activity. Rain, as well as dusk and dawn, pulls bass to the outside edge of lily pads.

SUMMER STRUCTURE

One of the reasons weeds are so beloved of largemouth anglers is that they're visible. Start thinking not only about the weeds themselves, but about the underwater structures they point to.

Irregularities in cover edges—Pockets and indentations in the weedline indicate differing bottom conditions.

Boat lanes—Where boats have carved out lanes within lily pads and other water weeds, preyfish like shiners hold along the weededges. When boats zip through, the fish scatter, triggering attacks by nearby bass.

Holes—Holes are a function of changes in bottom depth or composition. They have north, south, east, and west sides. When the sun's position shifts, bass may move from one to another side of holes, as well as from the outside to the inside of the hole.

THE TEN COMMANDMENTS
FOR WEEDEDGE BASSIN'

According to *In-Fisherman* co-founder Al Lindner, 10 percent of the weed areas hold 90 percent of the fish. Here are Al's tips for maximizing your success along weededges:

1. *Concentrate on weedlines with jagged edges.* Simple math: Broken weedlines have more bass-holding surface area, and active bass are out there, working the points to find prey.

2. *Fish troughs.* These are narrow channels that commonly run at a right angle to the shore. In reservoirs, they're often creek channels; on natural lakes, they may be dredged boat channels. In all cases, they're deeper than surrounding bottom, and bass move through them as if they were funnels connecting deeper water to shallow flats. Good troughs can produce fish throughout the day. Catch a few, leave for a few hours, and come back for the new fish that have moved in. Work troughs from deep to shallow. On natural lakes, these holes may be found close to the outside weededge, where they form saddles, one of the best types of structural element on natural lakes.

3. *Fish humps.* Humps are the mirror images of holes. They may be bald on top, offering inside edges as well as changes in depth. The farther offshore a hump is, the longer it takes bass to colonize it after the Spawn Period. If you pull many fish off of a hump shortly after the Spawn Period, it won't be good again for weeks, maybe even longer, so go easy.

4. *Don't forget weedless flats.* So far, we've talked mostly about weedbeds. Don't ignore large open flats, once midsummer arrives. They offer more area to support large schools of shad and bass. Check the edges of flats: humps, clumps, holes, pockets, and points often attract schools of summer bass.

5. *Don't pass up clean lips.* Weed-growth typically ends with a distinct drop-off. Sometimes you'll instead find a gradual slope that drops off dramatically at about 15 feet. The area between the weededge and the break constitutes a clean lip. Clean lips aren't common, but they're always worth seeking out. Often they're covered with bluegills. Bass feed on the lips, then retire to hold in thick weedcover.

Lush green vegetation provides oxygen, cover, and food to keep big bass happy.

Fishing on the Edge

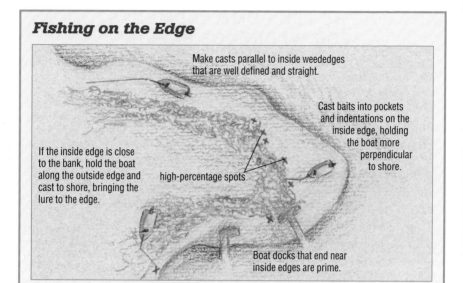

Make casts parallel to inside weededges that are well defined and straight.

Cast baits into pockets and indentations on the inside edge, holding the boat more perpendicular to shore.

If the inside edge is close to the bank, hold the boat along the outside edge and cast to shore, bringing the lure to the edge.

high-percentage spots

Boat docks that end near inside edges are prime.

6. *Identify weed walls and patch edges.* Weededges that grow from bottom to surface, parallel to a break, are called weed walls. Some weed species form walls along drop-offs where bottom type is consistent—for example, broadleaf pondweed, hydrilla, and milfoil. Others, like curly pondweed, coontail, and spiny naiad, are more likely to grow in clumps. Clumps are common where depth change is gradual and bottom type varies from silt to gravel. You can spot these with polarized sunglasses. Patchy weedlines commonly hold more bass than weed walls, but both are worth fishing.

7. *Fish points and pockets.* Watch for tufts of weeds outside the edges of a weed wall. These can be hard to spot, because tufts may grow only 4 or 5 feet off bottom. Sometimes you'll find weed tufts outside straight weededges, too. Such phantom weededges can be fantastic bass magnets. They allow active bass to move to the mouth of the pocket to feed and then retire to its back end, so they're never far from cover. The best pockets are long and narrow or rounded, and they always have narrow mouths.

8. *Try inside edges.* In midsummer, many bass anglers abandon the shallows, particularly inside weedlines. But bass continue to feed on shallow flats when the light is low. Prey, including spawning sunfish, and schools of shiners are still abundant in 2- to 4-foot sandy areas with sparse sandgrass or reeds, so largemouths remain nearby, too. On calm summer days, they also may visit inside edges looking for food. Locate inside edges at least 4 feet deep if the water's clear and 2 feet if it's murky, and you're likely to find bass.

9. *Be attentive to weather.* Stable weather means increased activity on the inside of weededges. But shifts in wind direction and blustery conditions can send bass into dense weedgrowth. After a front passes through, the action's in the deep weeds.

10. *Fish where edges end.* When you spot an opening in a weededge, it's usually there because of a change in bottom type. Breaks in weedlines draw bass from surrounding flats that are interested in intercepting preyfish. Fish them carefully and repeatedly.

DOCKIN' BASS

Postspawn bass are fairly easy to locate in the weedy natural lakes of the North, says Rick Lillegard, a longtime New England guide and winner of two B.A.S.S. tournaments: "In our part of the country, largemouths are quite predictable in their location. Despite increasing vegetation in recent years, we still look for the fish near docks. Docks can be key during the Postspawn Period. We have lots of permanent docks because our water doesn't fluctuate much."

A Dock-Fishing Bill of Rights

Lakeshore dwellers and anglers continually haggle over what's legally and ethically acceptable behavior. Ethics have little to do with this controversy. Most problems stem from lack of etiquette, the conventional requirements of social behavior.

Laws pertaining to lake access and ownership of shoreline areas, docks, lakebeds, and water vary among states, provinces, townships, and other political entities. Water regulatory agencies like the Army Corps of Engineers set rules for impoundments they create.

Knowledge of legal aspects is a necessary step in minimizing confrontation. But even more important is a code of standards for dock fishing situations.

Soc Clay

Fishermen
• Respect that the owner of the dock has spent time and money building and maintaining its structure. If the owner or guests are fishing from it or swimming around it, skip that dock.

• Avoid careless casts that might hit and possibly damage property such as fishing or swimming equipment, lights, or boats.

• Do not litter waters with paper, cans, cigarette butts, or plastic lures.

• Do not climb onto docks or private shorelines unless it's absolutely necessary. Attempt to free snagged hooks from on board.

• Do not leave hooks snagged on decks or ladders where they may be stepped on.

• Do not create a disturbance near occupied homes during sleeping hours.

• Observe no-wake areas near docks, even where they're not posted.

Dock Owners
• Understand that fishermen have a right to fish any water in the lake. Do not attempt to stymie their efforts by hanging lines, cables, or screens above the lake bottom, except where they're necessary to anchor boats or swim floats, or to secure other objects.

• Do not verbally harass anglers or create a disturbance.

Apply common sense—it reduces friction, making fishing more fun.

Secret Sweet Spots

Dock lights and pole holders suggest the dock owner planted brush as fish attractors.

dock lights

pole holder

pole holder

rope may be visible

boat slip

Styrofoam

Styrofoam log

2'

Christmas trees or other brush

● bass

Piece of steel used to reinforce the boat slip, 2 feet to 4 feet below the surface—bass often suspend by this.

Sunny-Day Docks

ramp

sunny

shade

sunny

gap

shade

● possible bass lairs

On a bright, sunny day, the best spots to pitch a jig to are shady.

sunny

sunny

In fact, largemouths may hold near or under docks continent-wide in all seasons except when ice forms. The number of docks on lakes and reservoirs has escalated dramatically since the 1970s. Bass use them as feeding stations, resting areas, and waypoints on longer migration routes. Largemouths first occupy the comfortable darkness beneath docks after they leave spawning bays. Females precede the males.

In a typical bay of a natural lake or reservoir, the fish-holding potential of docks varies. In summer, long docks that extend over deeper water provide the depth and cover that draw the greatest number of bass. But they're also fished more heavily than other kinds of docks. A seldom-fished, rickety dock over a shallow flat, on the other hand, can produce a lunker—because, on barren flats, docks provide largemouths with the only cover they're going to find. Docks on points attract groups of bass moving around a reservoir. Factor in such variables when you go dockin'.

Windy Docks

calm

calm

calm

Like the sun, wind affects the location of bass near docks.

With waves hitting the dock, largemouth and Kentucky bass should be on the windy side of the dock at a corner or gap in Styrofoam logs.

wind

gap

As summer progresses, the number of bass using docks increases after smaller bluegills, shiners, shad, perch, and other preyfish gravitate there. As the number of hot, sunny days grows, bass spend more time beneath docks than ever. Unhappily for you, on hot days in clear water, they tend to hold to the dark rear of docks, where traditional casting techniques can't reach them.

BASS BEYOND THE BREAKS

When summer sets in with 90°F days and blistering sun, bass not only move under the cover of docks but out into deeper offshore structure. Sometimes this may be a stumpfield or a single brushpile—or it may be a lengthy ledge abutting a creek channel 20 feet deep. "During midsummer, bass are more predictable than they've been since the spawn," says Texas pro Alton Jones, a former guide on Richland-Chambers Reservoir and a two-time B.A.S.S. winner. "It's structure fishing at its best. The guys who have trouble catching fish in summer need to learn how to fish structure, particularly drop-offs.

"When I was learning to fish structure, I'd read about people fishing drop-offs, but I didn't know if I was supposed to be fishing at the bottom of the drop, in the middle, or on top. Ninety-nine percent of the time, active bass will position right on that upper lip of the drop-off."

Twenty-five years ago, when Buck Perry devised spoonpluggin', he changed a lot of anglers' minds about what constituted favored structure for largemouths. Before then, structure was defined as weeds and timber. Supposedly, bass weren't to be found beyond these. Today, from the natural lakes of Minnesota to the bass-powerhouse impoundments of the South, it's still a minority of anglers who focus on offshore patterns. Those few often enjoy extraordinary fishing.

When bass finish spawning, most of them shift deeper. The deepest most anglers are willing to consider is the outside of the weededge, which commonly runs 12 to 15 feet deep in most waters. Many of the biggest fish, however, move well past woodgrowth and spend their summers in depths thought to be more typical of walleyes and smallmouths.

During midday in the Summer Period, bass often move to rocky, gravelly, or sandy humps, points, and deep flats. You won't find them there earlier in the day, but once the sun is high, you'll often find big bass deeper—and they're ready to bite.

Watch your flasher or graph closely. Liquid crystal units with long screens display features over a stretch of bottom which can help you interpret deep structure. Your unit needs to be powerful enough to show multiple echoes, which bounce readily off hard bottom. Sonar signals penetrate silt, and the echoes disappear when you move from hard to soft bottom. Learning to interpret these electronic readings is key to locating bass beyond the breaks.

When you graph a hump and see fish on bottom near rocks or stumps, you're probably locating largemouths that are in a feeding mood. Isolated rockpiles are ideal locations for offshore bass, especially if few such spots exist in that body of water. Where rock is more common, the best spots have plenty of vertical rock-cover, like boulders and slabs. If the rock is located on points, inside turns, or along doglegs, that's a plus. Get ready for action. If bass are holding a few feet off bottom, they're probably inactive and harder to catch. Move on.

WHY ARE BASS IN THE DEPTHS?

Prey is one of the biggest reasons. In many bodies of water, crawfish stay near bottom in deep water. And by midsummer, several baitfish species have also headed into deeper water. Others, like shad and alewife, school in open water and bass attack them off humps and deep points. Big bass follow them. Protection is another reason: Bass in these spots are seldom bothered by anglers. Oxygen levels are generally higher in cooler, deeper water, too, as long as you stay above the thermocline.

When the sun goes down, big bass prowl. So should you.

NIGHT FISHING

By midsummer, daytime temperatures push 100°F in the Southeast and Central states. Bass become less active in midday; fishing action shifts to early and late in the day. This is the time of year when night-fishing for big bass comes into its own.

Nocturnal bass can be frustrating to locate. They're out there somewhere, but the somewhere is big and often featureless. Where to start?

Look for structure associated with major tributaries, particularly deeper points at the mouths of tributaries, close to their intersection with the main lake or a creek channel. Current adds oxygen, attracts baitfish like threadfin and gizzard shad, and stimulates bass activity. Be sure to fish points to their maximum depth, provided that isn't below the thermocline, where there's little oxygen. Follow points out to 15, 20, 30 feet, and thoroughly probe the tips of those points.

Night-hunting bass move shallower, too, often hunting around humps. The best humps have at least 10 feet of water above them and include two or more elevations, with deeper saddle or razorback depressions between them. Fish can be found on the steep sides of these humps. The more gradual sides of these humps leading to deep water can be tremendous bass collectors in hot weather, because baitfish use these sides as links between shallow and deep water.

Big bass that suspend during summer move shallower after dark, to feed along the edges of weedlines or brush in the 8- to 12-foot range. They patrol favorite parts of coves and points, flushing prey until dawn sends them offshore again.

Bass often move to relatively open flats after dark, flushing bluegills, perch, and other prey that aren't as well equipped as the largemouth for night activity. Work open pockets between thick cover to catch them. Night fishing typically offers four distinctive bass activity periods:

Dusk bite—Bass that have been lurking in emergent and deep weedbeds shift to the edges. Those active during this period stop feeding when twilight turns to darkness.

Two hours after dark—Bass move from edges to open areas that don't hold fish by day. Sparsely weeded flats beyond lily-pad beds can be very productive. Shallow humps, bars, and cleared swimming areas are these nighttime basses' feeding grounds. It takes a bass almost an hour to switch from day vision to night vision, a physiological shift in the retina.

Middle of the night—This bite typically lasts about 45 minutes to an hour, occurring in open locations where bass were active an hour or two before sundown.

First light to sunup—Bass typically return to weededges, though a few remain in open pockets and over humps for an hour or more, taking advantage of the higher light-levels to feed. If you're planning on fishing by day, this is a great period during the hot weeks of the summer.

Summer never seems long enough! In the next chapter, we'll take a look at the largemouth's locations in the fall.

Fall Locations

TRANSITION TIME

The season we commonly call "Fall" includes two distinct subsections of the period during which water temperatures descend to their annual lows. The first phase begins with cooler nights and crisp days that may climb into the 70°F range but lack the feel of summer. In Minnesota, such conditions may begin in late August, while in Alabama, it may be in mid-October.

Gradual cooling coincides with shorter days that somehow signal many fish species to feed actively. In warmer regions, water temperatures have fallen from the excessively warm range into the optimal range for bass, crappie, walleyes, sunfish, and other species. In northern waters, an instinct must exist that urges bass to feed heavily in preparation for a long winter of near starvation. Largemouth bass feed actively for longer periods as waters cool, and they're eager to strike large lures.

Increasingly cool fall weather further cools surface waters, and their density increases with the drop in temperature. Eventually it becomes heavy enough to mix with the cooler, deeper water of the thermocline, on which the surface layer has floated since stratification began in summer. Though cooling alone can bring about the fall turnover, more often stormy, windy days bring turbulence that enables the entire lake to mix, an event called "fall turnover." Once water temperature has become more or less uniform from top to bottom, turnover is complete.

Not coincidentally, the crowds and boats have left on many lakes and reservoirs, and many anglers have morphed into land hunters. You may have the water to yourself. Chances are excellent that if you stay with fishing through fall, you'll encounter the largest—and the largest number of—bass for the year.

Throughout the largemouth's range, turnover narrows down the fish's optimal locations. Fish crowd into those areas that offer them what they had in such abundance throughout summer: cover, prey, and protection from other predators.

SEASON-WIDE LOCATIONS

In reservoirs, three locations transcend the particulars of early, mid-, and late fall—roadbeds, creeks, and rivers. We'll look at these first.

ROADBEDS

Throughout the fall after turnover, largemouths feed along deep roadbeds across their range, in reservoirs from New York to Texas. The mixing or oxygenation of surface and deep water creates an underwater free-for-all, allowing prey and predators access to all depths.

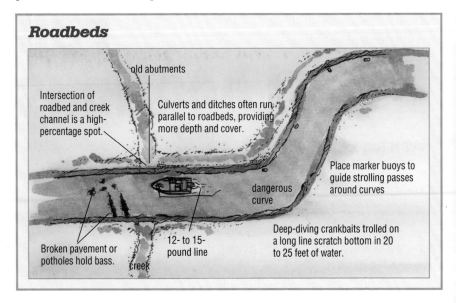

Roadbeds

Intersection of roadbed and creek channel is a high-percentage spot.

old abutments

Culverts and ditches often run parallel to roadbeds, providing more depth and cover.

Place marker buoys to guide strolling passes around curves

dangerous curve

Broken pavement or potholes hold bass.

creek

12- to 15-pound line

Deep-diving crankbaits trolled on a long line scratch bottom in 20 to 25 feet of water.

Largemouths group to attack baitfish at turns, intersections, dips, rises, bridges, stone walls, and culverts on submerged roadways. In these drowned landscapes, ranging from 10 to more than 30 feet deep, you'll find one of the most consistent fall patterns that lasts till lakes hit their annual lows.

CREEKS

Roadbeds aren't the only submerged structure that attracts bass. Also look for creek arms, because those also attract preyfish and bass.

Cooling water in fall pulls baitfish and bass from the mouths of tributaries and into the lower end of creek arms. In summer, these are warm and stagnant, their resident bass sluggish and few in number. The fish are easy to spot, come fall: Compared to the pale green, chunky lake fish, the creek fish are skinny and dark.

In midfall, submerged weeds in creeks start to thin, except for the deeper clumps of coontail and hydrilla, which attract groups of bass. Once water temperature falls below about 50°F, shad and bass leave the shallow ends of creek arms again and drop back toward the main reservoir.

During the Coldwater Period, creek-arm fish overwinter in the lower ends of large creeks that have little current.

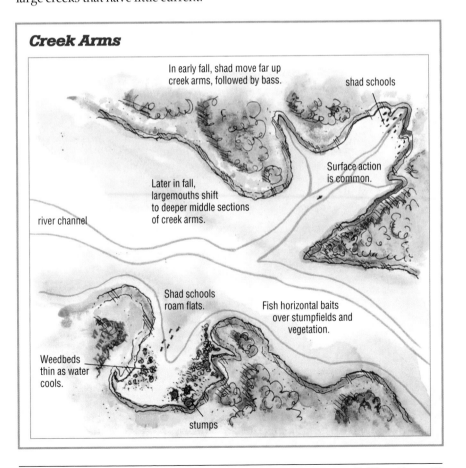

Creek Arms

In early fall, shad move far up creek arms, followed by bass.

shad schools

Surface action is common.

Later in fall, largemouths shift to deeper middle sections of creek arms.

river channel

Shad schools roam flats.

Fish horizontal baits over stumpfields and vegetation.

Weedbeds thin as water cools.

stumps

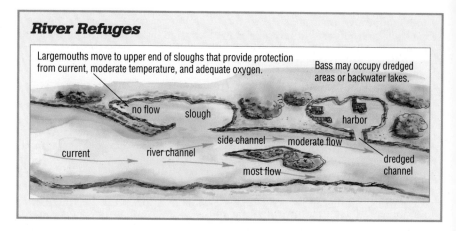

River Refuges

Largemouths move to upper end of sloughs that provide protection from current, moderate temperature, and adequate oxygen.

Bass may occupy dredged areas or backwater lakes.

no flow

slough

harbor

side channel

moderate flow

current

river channel

dredged channel

most flow

RIVERS

Largemouth bass typically avoid substantial current. They use it three seasons of the year if they need to, but come midfall and with the slowing of their metabolism, they seek out locations that shelter them from it. Tracking studies on several major rivers, including the Hudson and the Mississippi, demonstrate largemouths' preference for deep, protected locations with adequate oxygen. Unfortunately for them, such sites are few and far between. On Pool 12 of the Mississippi, for example—a 15-mile section partitioned by locks and dams—only three prime largemouth wintering locations have been found. On the Hudson, in the 100-mile tidal stretch below Troy, NY, only five winter refuges have been identified.

Typically, bass seek out the upper ends of deep sloughs, protected sections of tributaries, and manmade harbors. In colder climates, they migrate to these locales before weather gets rough—mid-September, in some cases. Elsewhere, they take shelter in side channels or backwaters until water temperatures fall into the low-50°F range, at which point they head into their wintering areas.

For largemouths in natural lakes and impoundments, the variables propelling movement are more complex. These can be divided into early, mid-, and late fall factors.

EARLY FALL LOCATIONS IN LAKES AND RESERVOIRS

The first phase of fall begins when water temperatures decline steadily, resulting in turnover. After turnover temperature may become constant, but everything else in the largemouth's world is now in flux: cover, weather, water temperature, oxygen level. Let's look at what these factors contribute to the largemouth's locations throughout fall. Learn these, and you'll be ready to find the biggest average-sized bass of the year.

COVER

When water grows cold, submerged plants along the shoreline thin out. As they decompose, they release phosphorus into the water, which fuels a bloom of phytoplankton. This carpet of microscopic plants shades the remaining weed-growth, increasing its rate of decline.

Apparently, the openings created as plants die back are great news to largemouths, which can now spot panfish and minnows more easily. Bass move into the shallows until water temperatures fall into the 40°F range, making use of the remaining bulrushes, maidencane, lily pads, fallen trees, and other visible cover, as sites from which to ambush and feed on prey.

Keep your eyes peeled for deeper-water plants once you no longer find largemouths in the shallows, because green weeds continue to key bass location. The two commonest weeds to persist in fall are pondweed and coontail.

Pondweed (Cabbage)—Plants of the genus *Potamogeton* are commonly called pondweed or cabbage. In fall, broadleafed varieties of pondweed typically can be found in 6 to 14 feet of water. In the northern half of the largemouth's range, the large-leafed pondweed, *Potamogeton amplifolius*, becomes the bass's preferred cover, as it survives long after shallower and less cold-tolerant plants die back. You can recognize *P. amplifolius* by its large arched leaves and dozens of distinctive veins; it shimmers in the depths on calm, sunny days.

Coontail—In some lakes, coontail *(Ceratophyllum demersum)* outlives cabbage in fall because it grows closer to bottom, where its short, crisp stalks form clumps anywhere from a hand's-breadth wide to as broad as a boat. Flashers indicate coontail clumps as wide red bands flickering just off bottom; liquid crystal sonar shows it clearly. Coontail still can reach the surface in fall in mature (eutrophic) waters, producing mats and stalks topped by broad, soft, dark-colored leaves (submerged plants are tighter and bright green, remaining so even when ice covers the surface). Bass hold just below these surface mats.

Both of these plants remain green long into fall in deeper water, with its more stable chemistry and temperature. Even in some northern lakes, small patches of luxuriant growth can be found as late as November, after the water temperature has sunk to the 40°F range.

WEATHER

Wind and rain seem to increase largemouths' feeding opportunities, probably since both roil the surface, increasing the bass's cover. If cold fronts drop water temperature fast, bass abandon the shallows for deeper water. Then they move onto beds of cabbage or coontail that remain green in deeper spots.

MID-FALL LOCATIONS

Once water temperatures fall into the 40°F to 50°F range (though some waters never reach this chilly temperature range), submerged vegetation thins even more. In the North, emergent plants like bulrushes, maidencane, cutgrass, and wild rice dry up and rattle. As their cover declines, bass begin congregating in the fewer remaining locations suited to them. This means slower fishing, until you find where they've concentrated. Then you can catch a bunch, but only by fishing slowly.

COVER

In natural lakes, inside turns that harbor the remaining cabbage and coontail patches concentrate largemouth bass, particularly when the plants are located on steep breaks near large flats. At this time of year, water temperatures in the shallows may fluctuate 5°F to 8°F between morning and afternoon. Largemouths shy away from such instability. Inside turns, with their more even temperature, draw bass. Weedbeds thrive there, enriched by silt and organic materials deposited from the shallows, and this living cover draws bass from points, humps, shallows, and other windblown structure. If a few large rocks are present or there's a change in substrate, even better. These remaining weedbeds provide cover and prey, even when the plants themselves are withering. In some dark, eutrophic lakes, even after plants have become reduced to black, slimy stalks in midfall, bass still hold next to them. Poor cover is apparently better than no cover at all.

In dark waters, bass may stay relatively shallow. Fish in clearer water—on sunny days with rising barometric pressure and/or rapidly falling water temperatures—sometimes shift deeper, past the stalks of the deepest weeds into 20 to 25 feet of water. Mild, sunny days with warming afternoon temperatures often pull bass shallow, where they hold in springtime spots like lily pads and fallen trees.

During mid-fall, bass abandon offshore humps, no matter how fine their weedgrowth. This pattern appears to be universal, once temperatures fall into the 40°F range.

Fall Transitions

Cooling water changes the aquatic environment and alters the behavior of largemouth bass and other fish. During early fall, bass feed shallow, deep, and in between, with the best locations depending on amount of cover, temperature trends, and time of day. Big bass hold near shallow cover that's close to deep water.

As fall progresses, shallow cover dwindles and more fish shift to remaining green weeds in deeper water. As ice-up approaches, bass hold along steeper drop-offs offering remaining weeds or other cover like stumps or rock. They shift vertically to feed on crayfish, occasionally moving shallow under mild calm weather. But cold fronts, wind, or falling temperatures move them past weedstalks into water over 20 feet deep.

Post Turnover—58°F to 50°F

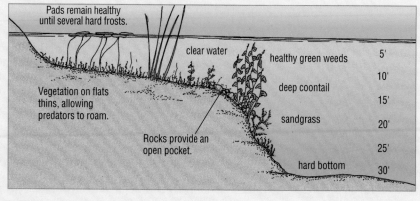

Pads remain healthy until several hard frosts.

Vegetation on flats thins, allowing predators to roam.

Rocks provide an open pocket.

clear water

healthy green weeds

deep coontail

sandgrass

hard bottom

5'
10'
15'
20'
25'
30'

WEATHER

Don't overlook wind direction when seeking mid-fall bass. Calm water and sun increase their activity. They rarely bite well on the windy side of the lake at this time of year. Moreover, the need to fish very slowly (even deadsticking baits) makes windy spots unproductive. As the water temperature approaches 40°F, the largemouth's metabolism slows significantly.

LATE FALL LOCATIONS

Bass are as concentrated as ever in remaining optimal locations after water temperatures drop toward 40°F, but their metabolism slows markedly. They are far less aggressive than in summer. Nevertheless, some of the finest fishing for big fish can occur weeks after the water dips into the 40°F range, as late fall doesn't change the largemouth's need for cover, stable water temperature (warmest available), and prey. Largemouths feed heavily in fall to fatten up for winter. Where their needs can be met they concentrate in great numbers, producing some of the best fishing of the year, particularly for the biggest bass on the lake.

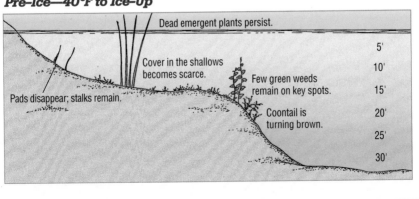

Midfall—50°F to 40°F

Pads wither.

Emergent plants turn brown.

Water darkens as decaying plants release phosphorus.

few stalks of green cabbage

Shallow vegetation dwindles; stalks remain.

Deep coontail remains dense.

5'
10'
15'
20'
25'
30'

Pre-Ice—40°F to Ice-Up

Dead emergent plants persist.

Cover in the shallows becomes scarce.

Few green weeds remain on key spots.

Pads disappear; stalks remain.

Coontail is turning brown.

5'
10'
15'
20'
25'
30'

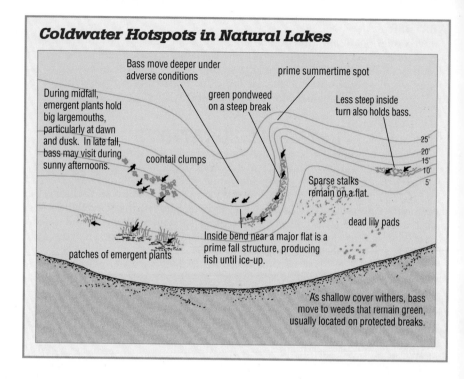

Coldwater Hotspots in Natural Lakes

Bass move deeper under adverse conditions

prime summertime spot

During midfall, emergent plants hold big largemouths, particularly at dawn and dusk. In late fall, bass may visit during sunny afternoons.

green pondweed on a steep break

Less steep inside turn also holds bass.

coontail clumps

Sparse stalks remain on a flat.

25'
20'
15'
10'
5'

dead lily pads

patches of emergent plants

Inside bend near a major flat is a prime fall structure, producing fish until ice-up.

As shallow cover withers, bass move to weeds that remain green, usually located on protected breaks.

COVER

Once cover has dwindled, largemouths gravitate to deeper rock or timber areas. The best flats are extensive, often more than 50 yards across from shore to the first break. Most taper gradually to 10 to 12 feet before breaking, a depth at which pondweed and coontail can be found into late fall. There, amid clouds of baitfish and mixed weeds, largemouths feed as far into the season as they can.

Below 40°F, largemouths show little inclination to move into the shallows. When they move, they can be found holding near the base of remaining weedstalks or along steep inside turns. At some point between late fall and ice-up on northern lakes, some largemouths move onto 20- to 30-foot-deep flats in the basins of bays, where they spend the winter beneath the ice. Often fish remain in vegetation as long as oxygen is sufficient.

In deeper reservoirs, bass favor vertical structure, such as bluff banks and deep outside turns on creek channels that offer stumps or standing timber. As water temperatures drop, largemouths hold deep, in the 18- to 35-foot depths in hill-land reservoirs, and deeper yet in highland or canyon impoundments.

The season has now reached the point where fishing with gloves and a warm parka is necessary. Next comes ice fishing. We'll examine the largemouth's winter locations in Chapter 6.

Frigid Fishing

Don Wirth

Winter Locations

LARGEMOUTHS AND STABILITY

Bass are conservative homebodies: They like to stick to their routines. They dislike rapid change. At no point is this clearer than in their winter behavior. You might think that winter works a hardship on them, since they're clearly such creatures of summer and warm water. But largemouths make it through the winter just as easily in northern Minnesota lakes covered with 3 feet of ice, as they do in southern Georgia lakes you can fish in December in shirtsleeves. Clearly these fish are a lot tougher and more adaptable than they appear.

Yes and no. Dr. Dave Philipp of the Illinois Natural History Survey explains why northern Minnesota bass get through winters that would kill southern bass, while southern bass make it through a summer that would finish off a northern largemouth: "The old phrase, 'A bass is a bass is a bass', isn't exactly true. We now know that a species is not a group of interbreeding creatures, but rather a collection of discrete stocks of fish. In the case of largemouth bass, these stocks vary greatly in their adaptations to diverse environments," he says. "In our experiments, the fitness of stocks—that is, their survival, growth, and reproductive ability—was optimal in their home waters and substantially reduced in alien environments. The only bass that survived in Minnesota were those from that region. Minnesota bass couldn't stand conditions in Texas or Florida. And even largemouths from Illinois didn't survive Minnesota winters."

What this means for anglers seeking bass in winter, whether on southern reservoirs, northern Minnesota natural lakes, or bodies of water in between, is that local fish are adapted to local winter conditions. You'll find them if you focus on the places that offer the greatest stability, even when that stability doesn't include the warmest water. They don't need the warmest water. They need water of the most constant temperature.

Rapid changes in environmental conditions, such as water temperature, oxygen content, pH, and water clarity, affect largemouths anytime—but particularly in winter. Researchers suspect this is because it takes longer for bass to adapt when their metabolisms are most sluggish, as they are in winter. They always favor stability over temporary conditions, even when those conditions seem more promising. Remember that places where conditions are likely to change for the better are also ones that are least resistant to changes for the worse.

In the North Country, winter bassin' calls for augers and ice rods.

To protect themselves against such sudden changes—for example, storms that alter water chemistry and clarity, or wind that creates surface-temperature fluctuations—bass congregate in areas that are most protected from such changes.

Notice that we didn't say protected from cold—your goal isn't to find areas most likely to warm up quickly if a sudden chinook howls through in January. To locate largemouths in winter, whatever winter means in your part of North America, you'll look for spots that will be the least affected by warming trends. You're scouting locations that are shaped by this paradox: The best fishing in winter can be found on lakes where most of the environment is harsh and where only a few small pockets exist that are less affected by changing weather.

When you find such spots, they'll contain lots of largemouths. These are loose aggregations, not schools of fish; individual fish that seek refuge in such places don't form a close-knit unit. Instead, they're creatures that have been driven to these few locations because conditions elsewhere are less hospitable.

Their average activity level is low. After early winter, bass rarely feed. Minnesota largemouths

The Power Plant Alternative

From Nelson Lake in North Dakota, to Fayette County in Texas or Georgia's Sinclair, warm water effluent from power plants fuels superb winter bass fishing. The surreal scene features falling snow while the superheated water creates an eternal plume of steam.

Hot ponds and canals draw baitfish of all sorts, and bass and other gamefish throng to the mild temperatures and plentiful food. Due to the unnatural temperature profile, power plant lakes also produce an early Spawn Period, preceded by an extended Prespawn Period that generally offers excellent fishing.

Power plants release their cooling water into ponds and canals, which then flows into the reservoir, creating a vast thermal plume whose size and temperature profile depend on the temperature and volume of water released. Bass and other fish select locations according to available water temperature and current, which can be strong near the release site.

In addition to hot winter-bass fishing, the extended growing season seems to spur outsized bass. Lake Monticello in Texas produced the former state record largemouth, while Fayette County is governed by a 14- to 24-inch protected slot limit to enhance lunker production. *In-Fisherman* cofounder Al Lindner favors Nelson Lake, producer of the North Dakota state record largemouth, for his open-water winter bass forays.

"I keep my crankbait rod spooled with fresh line all winter," he says, "as the bass often suspend in the thermal plume. Swimming a jig is another top option." On more southerly impoundments, topwater fishing with poppers and buzzbaits is possible over the Christmas holidays.

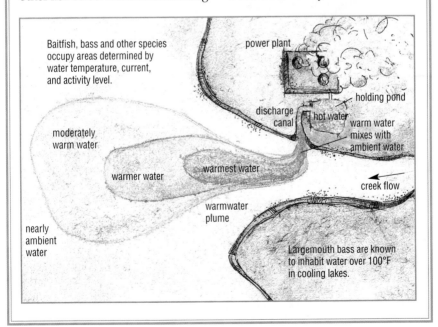

Baitfish, bass and other species occupy areas determined by water temperature, current, and activity level.

power plant

holding pond

discharge canal

hot water

warm water mixes with ambient water

moderately warm water

warmer water

warmest water

creek flow

warmwater plume

nearly ambient water

Largemouth bass are known to inhabit water over 100°F in cooling lakes.

taken through the ice in midwinter commonly have stomachs empty and shrunken to the size of walnuts, while telemetric studies of bass in North Carolina reservoirs have found some bass displaying no detectable movement between early January and the end of March. Even in Texas, largemouths' eating activity falls off dramatically as temperatures drop in winter. In one study, between temperatures of 68°F and 50°F, Texas bass ate from 1.5 to 2.6 percent of their body weight three times a week. Between 50° and 36°F, they ate only 0.5 to 1.5 percent of their body weight and only once every 5 to 7 days. Sudden cooling drastically cut their feeding activity.

Typically, bass wait it out until water temperature and other environmental conditions signal the beginning of spring. Whether spring means ice-out on northern lakes, or the return of water temperatures to the 50°F range farther south, it's the stability of such changes that signals the return of spring for largemouths, not a warm day here and there.

WHAT'S 'STABLE'?

Deep water—Environmental stability is usually provided by deep water. Look for areas where the angle of the drop-off increases and the amount of nearby shallow water decreases. Steep bluff banks that reach to the river channel are hot spots in many reservoirs. In some natural lakes, sharply sloping shorelines or points that reach the main basin are key areas, especially if they're adjacent to prime summer areas.

Lack of current—Current brings fluctuations in water color, clarity, and temperature and, as these spell higher energy expenditures for bass in winter, they'll avoid it. In reservoirs and rivers with strong current, look for winter bass in deep backwaters. If there aren't any, search out the best combination of reduced current and depth that you can find. Subject to their environment, bass settle for the best of what's available.

Springs—Springwater is usually constant in temperature and chemistry. Because of this, it represents an oasis of stability to bass in winter. Spring holes can be hard to find; look for spots in large bodies of water that don't freeze over or that ice-out quickly in spring.

Hard-bottomed—In natural lakes, some hard-bottomed points extend well past the weededge. These spots attract a variety of species including largemouth bass.

Guide and In-Fisherman contributor Jim Duckworth enjoyed sensational bass fishing in 37°F water, catching fish on crankbaits at Percy Priest Reservoir, Tennessee.

Don Wirth

STABLE LOCALES IN WINTER

NORTH COUNTRY PERSPECTIVES

In most of Minnesota and the central provinces of Canada, December brings early-ice conditions, winter's most favorable time for locating largemouths through the ice. Underwater cameras on Minnesota lakes show small groups of largemouths slowly meandering along the weedline, occasionally swimming into the tattered remains of coontail, or dropping off the break into water deeper than 12 feet. They're far from the lethargic creatures described in some popular and scientific reports, although water is already in the mid-30°F range. But they aren't much interested in feeding. In fact, the few feeding studies on bass under ice suggest they don't feed at all.

The best bass days tend to be mild and sunny, with steady or slowly falling barometric pressure.

Largemouth locations in northern natural lakes may differ from those in reservoirs because natural lakes contain more weedgrowth than most reservoirs do. Where sufficient weedgrowth exists, bass congregate in small areas such as inside turns and points with remaining weedcover. In reservoirs that lack substantial vegetation, bass drift from creek arms toward the mouths of the creeks. If cover in the form of logs and timber is present, particularly on inside bends, this concentrates bass the way weeds do. Whatever the cover type, it's key in winter. By ice-up time, 25 out of 50 fish may be concentrated in one prime spot, especially if it's where cover meets deeper water. In the North, winter can be divided into four phases:

- *First-ice,* when bass can be aggressive biters, though they may not eat again for another week.

Small Impoundments in Winter

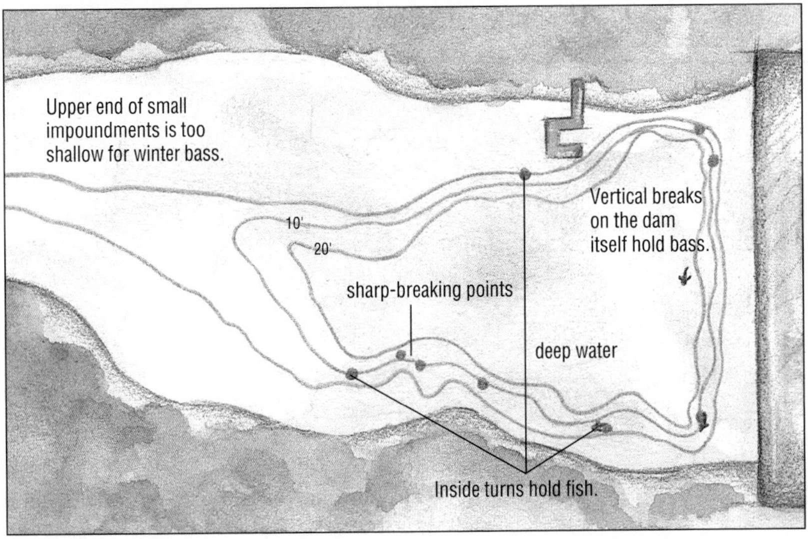

Upper end of small impoundments is too shallow for winter bass.

10'

20'

sharp-breaking points

Vertical breaks on the dam itself hold bass.

deep water

Inside turns hold fish.

- *Midwinter,* when bass hold in the most stable habitat they can find, moving little unless forced to by declining water quality, usually reduced oxygen.
- *Late-ice,* when bass become active and start drifting toward the bays and backwater areas they'll use just after ice-out, following minnows and panfish that have become active.
- *Ice-out,* when bass begin to move shallow again to seek cover and warmer water, and slowly resume feeding. After ice-out, when water temperatures rise to the low-50°F range, largemouths begin congregating on shallow flats or in bays, in 1 to 3 feet of water. They can be easily caught at this time.

REGIONAL VARIATIONS

Atlantic Coast—A few hundred miles to the south of Minnesota, and east along the Atlantic Coast, bass are typically quite active in small ponds and lakes in winter. Perhaps the shorter winter season exerts fewer constraints on their activity and feeding. The best bass days tend to be mild and sunny, with steady or slightly falling barometric pressure. When clouds veil the sun and snow begins to fall, a minor flurry of activity may commence. Dawn and dusk periods, however, won't stimulate activity in winter largemouths.

Winter Bass Movements

Many telemetry studies have investigated largemouth bass movements but, until recently, none had examined the activities of bass through winter in waters north of Florida and Mississippi. Dr. Rich Noble and Karle Woodward of North Carolina State University radio-tagged 11 adult largemouths in E. B. Jordan Reservoir in the Piedmont region of North Carolina, following them from late October into May.

The bass were captured and tagged in a single 23-foot-deep bay formed by a tributary creek. Ten bass remained there during the study, though 7 made occasional forays outside the bay.

Water temperatures during the study ranged from 69°F in late October to 42°F in late December, before warming to 71°F by late April. At normal pool the bay has sparse cover, consisting of sparse vegetation, small stickups, tree roots, and undercut banks.

As water cooled in fall, largemouths reduced the size of their home ranges. One bass showed no detectable movement from early January through the end of March. It wintered in tree roots at the

Central Region—In the swath from Virginia and North Carolina to northern Arkansas and Oklahoma (also in Oregon, for climate reasons), bays occasionally freeze but open water prevails all winter. Telemetric studies on the E. B. Jordan Reservoir in North Carolina indicate that bass have separate home ranges in winter from those they use in spring, summer, and fall. Locating them in this region often depends on finding schools of shad, which hold mostly in the main basins of reservoirs, where they can be thick enough to black out sonar screens. Early in the morning, shad are closer to the surface, shifting deeper around noon—down to 50 feet, at times. During cold snaps, shad cluster at about 10 feet, often over 25 to 50 feet of water. When water temperatures drop into the low-40°F range, threadfin shad go into shock and begin dying: When these shad bob to the surface or float into the depths, largemouths go on a feeding binge.

Guide Jim Duckworth of Tennessee has witnessed and fished a rare event, the 2000-2001 ice-up of J. Percy Priest Reservoir in Tennessee. He discovered that fishing on this 16,000-acre reservoir in 36°F to 39°F water was sensational. The bass were concentrated in 2 to 10 feet of water and feeding, apparently due to a major die-off of threadfin shad. Even on the coldest days of that unusual winter, Duckworth caught between 20 and 60 bass, thanks to the feeding frenzy catalyzed by expiring shad.

base of an undercut bank. Bass also shifted farther offshore during the coldest period that ended in mid-February. When water temperature climbed in February, the fish abruptly moved close to the bank.

During winter, largemouths tended to move closer to the bank in the early morning, shifting offshore from about 11 a.m. to 3 p.m., then approached the shore again in the late afternoon, where they remained at night. Once water temperatures rose in spring, the bass stayed near shore both day and night.

When water levels rose 6 inches or more, bass entered areas with flooded shoreline bushes and trees. They moved into such cover during the day and at night, though the shift was most pronounced in fall, late winter, and early spring. Some fish moved into flooded shoreline cover at water temperatures as low as 43°F.

Several of the largemouths established separate home ranges during winter, returning to those they'd used in fall when the water warmed—a behavior that previously had not been documented in adult largemouths, though noted for sub-adult bass. As other studies have shown, individual bass choose home ranges and faithfully return to them, though one bass in this study was a wanderer and didn't establish a home range at any point. Several fish moved to suspected spawning locations and remained there late into the tracking period.

Interestingly, the trackers followed the signal of one bass to an angler's livewell, where the sublegal fish (Jordan with a minimum-length limit of 16 inches) was residing. The angler released the bass.

*Woodward, K. O., and R. L. Noble. 1997. Over-winter movements of adult largemouth bass in a North Carolina reservoir. Proc. Annu. Conf. Southeast Assoc. Fish and Wildl. Agencies 51:113-122.

Coldwater Facts

I n the North, it's ice from December to April, sometimes even May. Ice imposes novel conditions on bass and anglers alike. Consider these ice facts:

- Current slows or prevents the formation of ice. In shallow, fast-moving streams, the only ice likely to form is on bottom—what's called anchor ice. Moving surface water often doesn't freeze at all, in these bodies of water.
- Ice is lighter than water, so 10 to 20 percent of it floats on the surface. For example, only 1 inch of a 20-inch layer of ice will be above water level. The weight of snow, however, can force ice down into the water.
- Lakes protected from wind freeze over faster than those exposed to wind. By midwinter, exposed lakes have more ice on them because wind reduces snow cover, which acts as insulation. Frigid air temperatures continually add more ice to the bottom of ice packs but, as the ice thickens, its rate of accumulation decreases.
- Ice serves as an insulator between the warmer water below and the colder air above.
- Snow is an insulator. When snow accumulates early in winter, before ice is thick enough to support fishing traffic safely, it can make the ice unstable all winter long—bad news for ice fishermen.
- Impurities lower the freezing point of water. Salt in ocean water, for example, lowers its freezing point from 32°F to 28.5°F. Similarly, northern waters, many of which are tannic and dark, actually freeze at a lower temperature.

The South—Some anglers believe that all bass hold deep in winter. They often don't. Look for them in the channel swings of tributary creeks along bluff banks on the outside bends, in water at least 8 feet deep. Where the bluff tails off, find where a shallow ledge drops vertically into the channel. Largemouths hold along these vertical rock faces. Rock is key for winter bass. If the sun is out, bass move into laydowns and stumps along steep banks in the afternoon.

Florida—A different set of conditions applies in Florida, where largemouths may spawn as early as December in the southern part of the state, January in central Florida, and February through early April in the northern part of the state. Winter is spawning season in Florida and bass stay shallow, remaining in cover near their nest sites.

Rocky Mountains—With the severest climate in the U.S., the Rockies aren't conducive to building largemouth populations. In several mountain states, only stocking keeps populations viable enough for fishing.

Pacific Coast—In California, introduced Florida bass become the biggest of that subspecies in the world, thanks to their inherent growth potential, the mild climate, and the rainbow trout (large and tasty prey for bass) with which they share so many waters. Giant bass are active and on the feed in California's reservoirs in winter when rainbows are stocked. Winter for largemouths on these waters represents an extended Prespawn Period fueled by a glut of trout, threadfin shad, and crayfish.

RESERVOIRS

Flatland and hill-land impoundments offer excellent bass habitat for all seasons and serve to illustrate some key winter patterns. In addition to the main river channel, reservoirs of this sort offer large tributaries with smaller feeders entering them, as well. Each new addition provides vertical options bass seek.

As winter sets in, bass settle into predictable patterns and locations that are based on structural options, prey position, and weather conditions. Mitch Looper, Barling, Arkansas, has built a strong reputation for catching bass—and lots of them—in extreme conditions. Looper favors times when few anglers venture out, either because they lack hope of success, or they'd rather not fish in bone-chilling cold nor endure heat indices over 120°F. The laconic Looper notes, "It's much easier for me to tolerate any weather conditions, than all the idiots out there when the weather is great."

Comparing summer and winter, Looper notes, "Bass often use the same structure in winter as in summer, or at least the same types of structure. But they hold deeper in winter." He's referring to the classic hill-land impounds of the Central and Southeast U.S., waters with well-defined channels, points, and creek arms, moderately clear to clear water, and little vegetation.

"Our best fishing in winter occurs with water temperatures between 42°F and 50°F, though I've made good catches in temperatures down to 38°F. The low-40°F range can yield sensational fishing in waters with threadfin shad. Shad start dying, and bass can't resist gorging on them, despite the cold water.

"Except during the spawn, points are always key in these reservoirs," Looper says. "But in winter, instead of holding right on the end of a point, bass more likely suspend 50 feet or so off the end of the point—say, 22 feet deep in 45 feet of water. During the Coldwater Period, wide, flat points rather than razorback structures seem to accommodate larger groups of bass.

"During winter, humps and creek channels are the other two key structures, and both have major vertical features. As with points, though, bass relate to them loosely, typically suspending not precisely at the drop-off but perhaps 12 to 60 feet off of it. Scouting with sonar is critical to quickly finding fish," he notes.

"Scan for schools of shad; that's what the bass are relating to. That's the one factor many winter bass fishermen miss. They target structure rather than shad. Oh, they pick up some fish, but not as many or as big as if they'd studied the way shad relate to structure, and fished accordingly."

Farther south, water temperatures rarely fall below 45°F. In Texas, southern Oklahoma and east to Georgia, hardy anglers make great reservoir catches right through winter (admittedly, avoiding the coldest snaps). Flatland impoundments are common, and they superficially offer less depth variation than the hill-land impoundments

In Florida, winter is prime time for lunkers.

Reservoirs

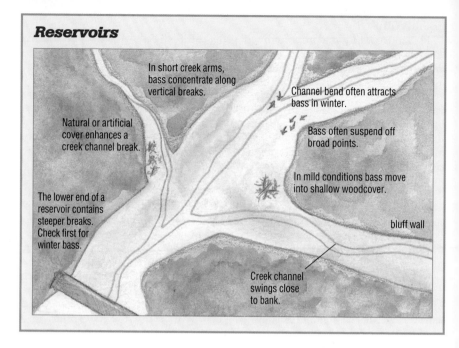

In short creek arms, bass concentrate along vertical breaks.

Natural or artificial cover enhances a creek channel break.

The lower end of a reservoir contains steeper breaks. Check first for winter bass.

Channel bend often attracts bass in winter.

Bass often suspend off broad points.

In mild conditions bass move into shallow woodcover.

bluff wall

Creek channel swings close to bank.

Mitch Looper targets. Creek arms and the reservoir basin are broader, creating extensive shallow and mid-depth flats with little vertical variation.

"That's what makes winter fishing so great," says Texas bass pro Alton Jones. By looking at a contour map, you can elimate at least 80 percent of the water. Because points in lowland impoundments usually aren't pronounced, I look for larger feeder creeks that still have sharp features—deep holes and channel swings that concentrate bass.

"I also look for bluff banks along the outside bend of the channel. Depth may be just 8 to 12 feet, but the other side of the channel may be just 3 or 4 feet deep. That's the kind of vertical feature needed to hold groups of bass.

"Bass favor vertical drops that offer shallow cover nearby," Jones adds. "During mild conditions, say a 50°F afternoon in January, bass move upward and bask in shallow water if the wind is light or calm. At night, they shift down the break, and in the morning, they'll be in the deepest holes."

In northern impoundments, bass positioning is similar during the final weeks before ice-up. In small impoundments, steep breaks near the dam hold bass. And wherever rock walls drop into creek channels, you'll find largemouth as well as smallmouth bass. In older northern impoundments, siltation and growth of submergent plants function more the way they do in natural lakes.

Chapter 7

Focus on Impoundments

Gord Pyzer

Reservoir Topics

WATERWAY CHARACTERISTICS

Reservoirs are the most varied of all largemouth bass habitats, ranging from small watershed impoundments to huge artificial lakes formed by damming major rivers. The watersheds from which reservoirs gather their water can be as small as several square miles or as large as a quarter of a million miles. Some reservoirs are largely riverine, with swift current that precludes thermal stratification. Others, particularly the largest, are wide and deep, their incoming currents small in proportion to the total volume of water. Reservoirs on small streams are likely to be clear and cold, while those behind big dams, because of the immense areas they drain, are frequently rich in silt and nutrients and murkier for longer periods than natural lakes.

Reservoirs are far less stable than natural lakes. They rise faster after heavy rains, sustain more dramatic changes in pH, and fluctuate more in volume. Their water levels don't merely reflect the rain levels of the surrounding watershed, but fluctuate with each dam's purpose: power generation, flood control, recreation, municipal water supply. Top all those factors with the bewildering variety of topography upstream and beneath reservoirs, and it's a wonder that any angler can master effective fishing on them.

On the bright side, reservoirs offer largemouths—and anglers—more bottom structure, shoreline cover, shallow, deep, and open-water bass habitat than most natural lakes. Reservoirs are worth study, since they produce outstanding fishing from New England to Mexico.

One man who's mastered the hidden character of reservoirs is Rick Clunn. With four Bassmaster Classic victories, two U.S. Open Championships, and a Red Man All-American title to his credit, Clunn has clearly learned how to find and catch bass in a hurry on reservoirs.

Rick Clunn, Ava, Missouri, has devised a system to quickly define winning patterns in reservoirs.

In-Fisherman followed Clunn on his quest to learn the secrets of Table Rock Lake, a 70-mile-long, 50,000-surface-acre reservoir in Missouri. Clunn was able to factor in the significant variables on a stretch of reservoir he'd never fished before, narrow down the range of likely water, and bring home the bacon. "You can't fish a 50,000-acre reservoir and expect to find fish the first day," he says. "But using the correct seasonal pattern will put you on the 10 percent of water where the bass are most active, which is much easier to cover in a few days."

What are Clunn's techniques? Depending on the time of year and where he's fishing, he determines what seasonal period (spring, summer, fall, winter) the reservoir's bass are in. Once he's identified this, he searches for areas on the map likely to attract bass during that season. By excluding nonproductive water, he can eliminate up to three-quarters of even the biggest reservoir surface area before he arrives.

RESERVOIR TYPES AND CHARACTERISTICS

In-Fisherman categorizes reservoir topography as lowland, flatland, hill-land, highland, plateau, and canyon. By identifying which terrain underlies and surrounds a reservoir, you can anticipate basic underwater structures, shoreline forms, and depths. *Bass Fundamentals,* our previous volume in the Critical Concepts series, describes in detail each reservoir type. Here, we'll address issues pertinent to largemouth locations.

RESERVOIR SIZE, SHAPE, AND DEPTH

Wide, shallow reservoirs warm quickly in spring, stratify early in summer, and cool rapidly in fall. They also silt up faster, remain murkier, and are more likely to be anoxic (lacking oxygen) near bottom than deeper ones. Seasonal changes, in other words, have immediate and sometimes drastic impacts on bass in shallow reservoirs.

Narrow, deep reservoirs warm up and cool down more slowly. Because of this, Spawn Period and Postsummer Period tend to last longer on them. In the South, deep hill-land and highland reservoirs may not cool down enough to enter a true Coldwater Period.

Even within these two basic categories, conditions vary depending on reservoir size. Small waters undergo complete water changes more quickly during rainy seasons, with less stable temperatures and chemical profiles.

Bass, as anglers know, like stability, so small reservoirs generally provide less consistent bass fishing than large ones.

FUNCTION

A dam's purpose tells you a lot about how stable its reservoir environment is. Water-level fluctuations are inevitable in reservoirs; the key question is whether or not they create instabilities capable of crippling the bass fishery. For example, water-level reductions expose banks to erosion and may wash away woody shoreline cover, sand, and organic material conducive to plant growth. Soft soils may drift into river channels, leaving shores rocky, weedless, and infertile. On reservoirs where water fluctuations are common, the food base is usually plankton, and bass must rely on pelagic preyfish such as shad or alewives. Clear reservoirs with dramatic fluctuations in water level are usually not very productive of bass.

Hydroelectric—Bass in hydroelectric-power reservoirs often match their feeding periods to power-generation schedules. Prey species like shad school tightly and are vulnerable in current, so bass often feed aggressively when generators are operating. Sunfish and crayfish, however, seek shelter from current. Where these are the dominant prey, bass may be more active when current is weak.

Dam generators operate when demands for electrical power are high. Peak generation tends to occur in hot months, when air conditioners are used heavily, and in midwinter, when days are short and electrical lights are in constant use. Demands are highest in the late afternoon and evening, so water levels may fluctuate accordingly on a daily schedule. Generation also is more consistent during the week than on weekends.

Flood control—Reservoirs built for flood control experience the most variable conditions by season. In spring, they may rise many feet above their summer and winter levels. High spring water levels often produce large hatches of bass, increase cover options, and protect bass from harvest. A single season of high water may improve fishing for years to come by helping young bass reach maturity. Timing of first hatches of largemouth fry on reservoirs is linked not to temperature, but to the first day on which water levels reach full pool, according to a study conducted on Tennessee's Normandy Reservoir. Largemouths grew faster and attained larger size during wet years, when full pool was reached in early spring and maintained for at least two months in summer. Bass survival was also higher in high-water years. Manipulating water levels by reaching full pool early in spring and maintaining it for 90 days on flood-control reservoirs like Normandy can play a significant role in building a successful fishery.

The downside to this is that constantly fluctuating levels often reduce spawning habitat. Bass in such waters tend to inhabit steep structures that extend from below the maximum drawdown depth to near full-pool level. These spots give them what they need—stability. In fluctuating impoundments, steep points and bluffs become prime locations.

Municipal water supplies—Reservoirs built to store water for municipal water supplies usually fluctuate less than those built for other purposes. Usually these are drawn down the most in summer and fall.

Reservoir Bass Survey

The Tennessee Valley Authority operates most of the major impoundments of the Midsouth, across Tennessee, Kentucky, and Alabama. Their fishery staff recently surveyed bass populations in the lakes by electrofishing.

In an interesting twist to the standard survey, biologists arrange for local anglers to fish the sampling area for an hour before they begin electrofishing. This provides an opportunity for the biologists and anglers to discuss fishing issues, as the anglers are invariably amazed at how many bass they don't catch.

In 2001, the catch rate of bass over 10 inches for the 13 reservoirs was about a fish a minute, slightly higher than the previous year, though the number of bass over 4 pounds declined. Guntersville, on the Tennessee River in northwest Alabama, and Fort Loudoun in Knoxville, showed strong increases over recent surveys. Wilson Lake on the Tennessee

River in Northeast Alabama had the highest density of bass, while Watts Bar in East Tennessee produced the biggest bass at 6.2 pounds. Guntersville featured the largest average size, 1.7 pounds.

For information on these surveys or to participate, contact the Tennessee Valley Authority at 865/632-1721, or *www.tva.gov*.

2001 Black Bass Survey Results

Reservoir	No. of Bass Per Acre*	Pounds Per Acre	Average Weight (lbs.)
Boone	7	6.24	1.3
Chickamauga	5	2.3	0.81
Douglas	5.1	2.9	0.92
Fort Loudoun	17.3	12.6	1.1
Guntersville	16.1	21.4	1.7
Kentucky	3.8	2	1.6
Melton Hill	1.4	0.54	0.85
Normandy	4.6	2.7	1.1
Pickwick	10.4	5.8	1
Tims Ford	1.1	1	1.3
Watts Bar	12.4	7.31	1.5
Wheeler	16.3	9.7	1.2
Wilson	18.2	11.9	1.2

*10 inches or more in length.

Irrigation—During dry seasons, irrigation reservoirs drain sharply because they're not replenished. Their levels usually drop in spring, when rains stop. Wet years refill such reservoirs, but extended drought can lead to drawdowns that damage fisheries.

Recreation—Most reservoirs are built for more than recreational purposes, but some of those that support fishing and water sports, as well, try to balance hydroelectric or irrigation needs against demands for fish spawning habitat, boat access, and current for activities like whitewater rafting or tailrace trout-fishing.

Where reservoirs have been built to support real-estate speculation, water levels tend to remain constant, producing excellent fishing for decades if prey and cover are abundant, harvest isn't excessive, and vegetation coverage is moderate. Eventually, however, shallow cover rots and shorelines become barren. Fixed-level reservoirs provide better fishing if their water levels are allowed to fluctuate sufficiently to flood terrestrial vegetation during and immediately after the spring Spawn Period.

When water fluctuations are common, the food base is usually plankton, and bass must rely on pelagic preyfish.

WATER LEVELS

Bass in reservoirs with annual drawdowns adapt to a suspended, open-water life or change their habitats seasonally. Shallow flats and banks with gently sloping bottoms frequently become too shallow to hold bass, vegetation, and prey. Exposed flats only attract migrant bass once they're reflooded.

Reservoir bass move shallower when doing so is advantageous. When water inundates shorelines covered with terrestrial vegetation, the new shallows often provide abundant food and cover that attract preyfish. In reservoirs with barren shorelines above the waterline, increases in water level usually provide little additional food or cover. In such reservoirs, bass are likely to stay at their accustomed depths.

Dropping water levels force bass off shallow flats and away from shoreline cover. But when sudden drops in water level force crayfish out of their holes, bass may temporarily rush back to the shallows to feed on them. Periodic drawdowns that don't lower water level enough to expose the outer edge of weedlines can reshape the inside edges of offshore weeds into distinct weedwalls.

Where reservoirs are subjected to occasional brief drawdowns, milfoil may come to dominate the vegetation. Long-term drawdowns of 5 to 20 feet, on the other hand, kill most exposed water-plants. The resulting deeper light penetration increases the likelihood that hydrilla and other deep-rooting species will colonize the now-empty water. Fall drawdowns may help bass fisheries by exposing prey sheltered in bays and along shorelines.

CURRENT

The ratio of incoming and outgoing water to reservoir volume, the shape of an impoundment, and the directional flow toward outlets determine where current can be found on reservoirs. Incoming water seeks its own density. Warm, "light" water flows into and mixes with warm surface-water. Cold, dense water sinks under the warm surface and mixes with cold water beneath the thermocline. Salty (mineral-laden) water, being heavier than pure water of the same temperature, sinks as well. Pure, warm rainwater floats on cold, heavier saltwater; cold rainwater mixes with warm surface-water while it sinks. All of these patterns produce discernible current.

Large, deep-draining reservoirs may develop variable temperature profiles and may not experience distinct fall turnover because their coldest water is continually drained off. Instead, the average temperature of their deepest water remains higher and their thermoclines deeper than those of shallow reservoirs. Incoming flows spread and dissipate, creating discernable current only in their upstream areas that receive water from the next dam. Such reservoirs generally provide stable environments and good bass fishing. In deep reservoirs that drain from the surface, shallow currents sluice off nutrients quickly, leaving relatively stagnant bottom water for months. Mediocre fisheries often result.

CLINES

Technically, clines are markedly different areas on graphs. To bassers, they are areas where characteristics of water change radically. Areas of rapid temperature change are called thermoclines. Similar interfaces occur between waters of differing pH (pH-clines), oxygen level (oxyclines), clarity (clarity-clines), and chemical properties (chemoclines).

Current mixes water horizontally and vertically. During part of the year, temperature and chemical content of reservoir water is fairly uniform and cline-free. But warm water is lighter than cool water, and the top few feet of reservoir water absorb the sun's heat. Unless that heated water is forced deeper, it will float on top of the colder water below it. Most reservoir thermoclines form at 15 to 30 feet below the surface, their exact depth depending on wind, temperature gradients and current. Knowing how deep these lie is a significant factor in locating bass.

Reservoirs are the most varied of all largemouth bass habitats, ranging from small watershed impoundments to huge artificial lakes.

Oxyclines form once thermoclines prevent the water below them from receiving new oxygen from the surface. Below thermoclines, living animals and plants use up the available oxygen, creating anoxic conditions. Bass require 5 parts per million (ppm) or more of dissolved oxygen to stay in good health. Water with less than 3 ppm in the hypolimnion, the condition of much reservoir water by midsummer, may prompt them to move.

The pH-clines form when dissolving organic material creates acidic or alkaline layers that drift in or slightly above thermoclines and oxyclines. Bass actively avoid acidic (pH less than 6) and high-alkaline (pH more than 9) waters.

Clines, in short, are important factors in locating bass in reservoirs, because clines form semi-permeable barriers to the largemouth's vertical and horizontal movement. The good news is that when they encounter clines, bass stop and concentrate. Good fishing is likely in such locations.

WATER CLARITY

Factors in water clarity and color are the presence and type of plankton, dissolved organic matter, and suspended particles. In long reservoirs, inflowing water may be turbid and stained, while water downstream near the dam is clear. Water clarity gradients can alter fishing conditions over the length of reservoirs and their long tributary arms.

Water clarity determines the maximum depth largemouths use in a reservoir. Bass usually occupy depths down to whatever depth light becomes too faint for plants or plankton to grow. Bass living in clear water may stop feeding whenever the water becomes turbid. But rather than abandon their accustomed home range, they're likely to wait out brief periods of turbidity. They can, and frequently do, go without food for days or even weeks without suffering ill effects.

Mud is another matter—bass try to move away from it. Where muddy water persists over several months, it can kill underwater vegetation by shading it. Once weeds have died, they may take weeks or years to return, depending on their species and on water conditions. This represents a radical change in the largemouth's world, and the fish are apt to resettle elsewhere.

In reservoirs where muddy water is common, largemouths adapt to it. Legendary angler and TV host Bill Dance has noticed that bass in muddy reservoirs appear to make greater use of their lateral lines to sense vibrations, in waters where their visual range is reduced by turbidity. They also hold closer to objects, seeking the security of docks, brushpiles, or boulders, perhaps using those objects as reference points. And because forage fish are affected by muddy conditions, which push them toward the shoreline, bass go shallower, too. Dance notes that bass commonly living in clear water are harder to catch when their habitat turns muddy, than are bass from water that's typically stained. Clear-water bass are used to feeding almost entirely by sight; bass accustomed to murky feeding conditions seem to rely more on their other senses to cope with reduced visibility. In muddy water, key locations for finding largemouths include:

Shallow points—Fish these far from the main river channel, yet close to deep water. The best often have bottom composed of pea gravel, shale, slate, chunk rock, or red clay.

Springs—Muddy and clear water mix wherever springs enter a reservoir. The area surrounding springs draws largemouths and their prey.

Rocky banks—Look for bass around gravel bars, riprap banks, and chunk rock in current. Large rocks deflect current and provide holding spots. Smaller rocks filter sediment from the water, clearing it quickly.

Pockets—Current flow is reduced along banks, no matter how shallow. Stumps or logs make such spots even better.

Shoals—Largemouths concentrate along the lower ends of shoals where current is reduced.

Manmade structures—Largemouths often hold in shallow spots near current edges or objects. Such spots also concentrate baitfish, especially where structures are adjacent to shallow, slack water.

Temperature and Altitude Affect Oxygen Content

At sea level, 50°F water can hold 11.3 parts per million (ppm) of oxygen at saturation, more than enough for any freshwater fish to thrive. Water at 90°F is saturated at 7.3 ppm, still sufficient for healthy free-roaming fish. But minnows in a bait bucket and bass in a livewell quickly consume all the available oxygen in warm water, becoming stressed and then dying. Altitude affects oxygen content, too. As altitude increases, water's potential to hold oxygen is reduced by as much as 20 percent.

Temperature (°F)	Altitude, Feet over Sea Level			
	0	1000	3000	5000
90	7.3	7.0	6.5	6.0
80	8.1	7.8	7.3	6.7
70	9.0	8.6	8.1	7.5
60	10.1	9.7	9.1	8.4
50	11.3	10.8	10.2	9.4
40	13.0	12.5	11.7	10.8

Oxygen Saturation (ppm)

VEGETATION

Weeds are neither good nor bad; like everything else in the largemouth's world, their value is variable. Because reservoirs are manmade and man-managed, however, the role of weeds comes more into question on these impoundments than it does on natural lakes.

Studies of public reservoirs in Texas show that the best bass fisheries develop in impoundments where vegetation covers up to 20 percent of the surface; but that's on big reservoirs. In small fishing lakes, well-managed, weed-free impoundments typically produce more fish. That's the case only when pond owners strictly limit the harvest of predators, however. Without harvest controls, weed-free ponds often contain only stunted, undersized fish.

We're going to focus our attention here on large impoundments. For the most part, vegetation in large reservoirs has positive effects: It provides protection for fingerlings, increases the number of small adult fish, provides the habitat favored by shoreline-oriented species like largemouths and bluegills, and increases the surface area of cover, thereby providing more habitat for algae, insects, snails, and shrimp—and the fish that eat them. Weeds clear murky water, filter out suspended sediment, and help to reduce the wave action that stirs up muddy shorelines. Because of their role in providing cover, weeds also help to limit overharvest of species like the largemouth, which make intimate use of their cover.

Let's take a brief look at how weeds have rejuvenated Sam Rayburn Reservoir, the famous Texas water that became an angling Mecca in the mid- to late 1960s.

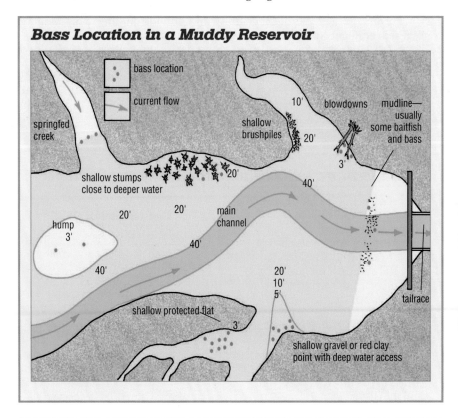

Bass Location in a Muddy Reservoir

bass location

current flow

springfed creek

shallow brushpiles

blowdowns

mudline— usually some baitfish and bass

10'

20'

3'

shallow stumps close to deeper water

20'

40'

hump 3'

20'

20'

main channel

40'

40'

shallow protected flat

20'
10'
5'

3'

tailrace

shallow gravel or red clay point with deep water access

Once its original tree and brush cover rotted away, fishing declined. That changed for the better in the late 1970s, when the lake was lowered 12 feet for a year and a half of dam repairs. This drawdown allowed buck brush, willows, and other trees and shrubs to germinate in the warm muck newly exposed to the air. When the reservoir's level rose again, the now-drowned vegetation seemed to revitalize "Big Sam." Exotic hydrilla, which formed an inside edge at about 7 feet along the drawn-down shoreline, spread far out into the lake, creating nearly vertical walls to a depth of 15 to 20 feet on their outer edge.

Rayburn's bass, particularly the lunkers, remain relatively shallow throughout the Coldwater, Prespawn, Spawn, and Postspawn Periods. From December to about mid-May, the inside weededge can be key to finding bass on Big Sam. They leave the shallower inner weededge only when lowering water levels and regrowth of the shallow hydrilla fill the inner edge. Later, thickening hydrilla forces bass to move to outer edges along open water, or to hold beneath the grass. Their outer-edge location persists until Rayburn waters rise again in December.

Bass usually occupy depths down to whatever depth light becomes too faint for plants or plankton to grow.

Before hydrilla arrived in Big Sam, bass held on structure 30 or more feet deep during winter. Now, Rayburn bass seldom leave the hydrilla or go deeper than 24 feet. And while the particulars of this Texas reservoir aren't precisely duplicated elsewhere, similar weedcover patterns have become critical to locating bass on many of North America's big reservoirs. Learn the ones that apply to your own favored reservoirs.

STRUCTURE

The terrain surrounding a reservoir tells you what types of structure lie beneath its waters. For example, nearby smooth and gradual rises suggest that the lake bottom is flat; flooded roadways and meandering creek channels characterize such substrates. Steep hillsides suggest straight-channeled creeks with plenty of drowned timber. Steep canyonlands suggest rocky, uneven bottom, and so on.

During their seasonal migrations, bass follow these submerged structures in reservoirs from deep-water wintering areas to shallow spawning flats. But thanks to tracking studies, we know that from the Prespawn Period through Postsummer Period, many lunker bass in reservoirs make limited movements of a few hundred yards. They hold at a depth of 8 to 18 feet on the outside of weededges, making forays closer to shore at sunset and feeding actively after dark.

Bass prefer weeds to drowned wood and shoreline vegetation. They seem to prefer native plants to exotics like hydrilla, which can easily grow out of control in reservoirs, choking out other growth. The water surrounding weedbeds typically holds more oxygen by day than adjacent areas, and bass prefer that, too.

Where weeds are scarce, bass are attracted to drowned wood, particularly thick, branched, horizontal wood. Wood, however, eventually floats or rots away—most trees periodically exposed to air disappear within 15 years. While it remains, however, wood provides good cover and feeding habitat.

Rock also offers cover for largemouth bass. It's primarily a feeding structure, providing holes and cracks from which crayfish, darters, shad and other preyfish can be captured. Boulders and slabs form feeding zones, while rock bluffs and riprap offer attractive and tough uniform cover. Look for small points, ledges or holes along these spots.

Largemouths typically prefer to spawn on bottom that's firm and protected from strong currents, boat traffic, and wind, and close to bulky cover. Not every reservoir offers such conditions, and adaptable bass will settle for what's available. You'll find them bedding over a wider variety of bottom in reservoirs than in natural lakes, including stumps, tree limbs and plant roots.

In summer, reservoirs offer a wide range of habitat for bass, and it becomes important to figure out where they're likely to hold. In highland impoundments, where creek channels are almost always deeper than bass typically use, largemouths tend to be point-oriented. They make heavy use of cover—weeds, stumps, standing timber—along the steep, rocky shorelines that characterize highland reservoirs.

In flatland reservoirs, main river channels are typically within range of bass. High spots along the edges of channels, as well as intersections with side channels, are summertime hot-spots. Ridges, rises, and creek intersections with heavy cover are also used frequently.

Weed Wars

S ome biologists claim that the exotic invaders, hydrilla and Eurasian water milfoil, are undesirable vegetation that should be eradicated. Bass anglers counter that this habitat is responsible for the recovery of bass fisheries in many aging reservoirs and that the best bass fisheries are those with reasonable amounts of vegetation. Biologists counter that vegetation isn't that important to bass fisheries.

Exotic weeds do make waters less usable to many recreational groups. But it's a leap of faith for biologists to conclude that exotics must be eradicated, when some studies suggest that bass fisheries may be most productive with 15 to 30 percent vegetation cover. They often argue, however, that this vegetation must be native plants, not exotics.

Several myths or distortions are involved. The first is that exotic weeds are controllable and that weed-control agencies need only have the authority and adequate funding to control them. In fact, both hydrilla and Eurasian water milfoil have proven adept at avoiding eradication. Total eradication is an unrealistic goal, and weed controllers should think about compromise solutions.

Another myth is that anglers "don't know what they're talking about." Many bass anglers have fished both weedy and weedless habitats, and their experiences typically have shown that weedy, if not excessively weedy, waters sustain larger bass populations and almost always provide better fishing than coverless waters. The 15 to 30 percent weed coverage cited by fishery biologists seems to correlate with the experiences of these anglers.

The typical bass anglers' view, however, is also a distortion. It is based on past observations of bass habitats and is valid for the past when few protective limits were applied. In the absence of protective limits, vegetation has protected bass from excessive harvest and has sustained fisheries. Weed eradication doesn't immediately reduce adult bass populations by killing fish, unless oxygen depletion occurs.

In hill-land reservoirs, bottom is the most varied of all. Manmade structures like submerged roadbeds, ponds and foundations often are key to summertime bass location on such impoundments.

In fall, decreased daylight, cool nights, and wind force reservoirs to turn over, releasing water from below the typically oxygen-deficient thermocline. This sudden change in water chemistry affects bass, and their activity level plunges. Look for submerged riverine locations where turnover isn't a factor. Move upstream in the main river arm or far back into a sizable tributary. Fish there will be scattered and cover-oriented. Early fall often brings a migration of shad into creek arms and bass follow. Look for points, channel turns or stump rows where bass typically attack the baitfish.

On reservoirs with fall drawdowns, bass move first into the shallows to take advantage of baitfish forced into the open by falling water levels and thinning vegetation. Afterward, however, usually following fall turnover, bass are forced

Removal does, however, change predator-prey relationships and balances. If competitive open-water predators like white bass, striped bass, and hybrids are present, eliminating plants can shift the balance away from a bass-bluegill fishery to a pelagic predator-shad fishery. And the bass population suffers. Bass can function as open-water predators if populations are maintained near capacity and bass don't have to compete with species more efficient in open water.

Also, many reservoirs have shortages of shallow cover, and increasing vegetation may be the least expensive and most efficient way to restore these fisheries. Weed controllers need to include the value of healthy fisheries in their decision-making process. Sometimes a good fishery is more valuable than open water for swimmers or lakeside homeowners.

Merlyn Hilmoe

When weed-control decisions are made, anglers' views as well as the feelings of lakeside landowners should be considered. Landowners should expect to live on a lake without transforming it into a swimming pool.

When weed-control biologists plan to partially or totally remove vegetation, part of their planning should involve coordinating with fishery managers to assure that black bass populations are immediately protected from increased harvest. Fishery managers must act quickly. Waiting until overharvest occurs and then trying to recover the fishery with a special limit is inefficient.

Ralph Manns

Habitat Separation of Black Bass Species

Biologists from the Tennessee Cooperative Fisheries Research Unit used electro-fishing to sample largemouth, smallmouth, and spotted bass populations in Normandy Reservoir, Tennessee, a TVA flood-control and water-supply impoundment.* The 3,200-acre lake has an average depth of about 35 feet at full pool, is drawn down about 15 feet in fall,

Kevin Brant

and returned to pool depth in spring. This "slick" highland lake offers only a few small coves, along with rock, rubble, and hard-bottom habitat for cover.

Samples were collected in the spring (March-April) and fall (October-November) for six years to see how the three bass species separated from each other in space and time. The most abundant habitat type was gravel (44%), with rubble (33%), mixed materials (11%), coves (8%), and riprap (4%).

In spring, our focus here, 688 largemouths, 173 smallmouths, and 686 spotted bass were captured. Largemouth were most abundant near riprap and in coves, and least abundant in gravel habitat. Smallmouths were most abundant near riprap, using all other habitat types sparingly. Spotted bass were most abundant in rubble habitat in two of six years, but were evenly distributed among all habitat types in four other years. Spotted bass were least likely to be found in coves.

Bass of all three species taken from gravel habitat were mostly young-of-the-year fish. Apparently, gravel was used as spawning or nursery areas by all three species.

The attractiveness of the scarce riprap to all three species indicates that larger rocks offered prime habitat, probably providing hiding spots for forage. The selection of rubble habitat by spotted bass in two of the six years may have been the result of concentrations of prey there that the spotted bass were adept at exploiting. Or it may also have been the result of the exclusion of some spotted bass from riprap by the larger largemouth bass.

The only habitat that offered diverse cover, the type normally used by black bass when available, were coves. Coves were dominated by largemouths in spring, apparently forcing larger members of the other species elsewhere. This domination of typical spawning habitat may have limited the overall numbers of the other bass species.

The results of this study contrast with older studies of the habitats used by these three species in Norris reservoir, where captures in nets revealed that the species tended to separate by depth, with largemouths shallow and spotted bass deep. Scarcer smallmouth used in-between depths and often schooled and fed in open water.

Most Abundant Bass Habitat Type	
Gravel	44%
Rubble	33%
Mixed	11%
Coves	8%
Riprap	4%

Ralph Manns

*Sammons, S. M. and P. W. Bettoli. 1999. Spatial and temporal variation in electrofishing catch rates of three species of black bass (*Micropterus spp.*) from Normandy Reservoir, Tennessee. N. Amer. J. Fish. Mngt. 19(2):454-461.

deeper, away from shallow flats and out of bays. The first major break or drop-off outside of shallow habitat offers them a coldwater refuge.

As the season progresses, the general upstream movement of spring is reversed and more bass move downstream, typically toward deeper water. The larger the volume of deep water, the less influence that short-term changes in weather have on bass. To locate them at this period, concentrate on the steepest breaks in deep areas.

Fifty thousand surface acres of reservoir may look featureless, but like Rick Clunn, you can learn how to find the 10 percent of water that yields 90 percent of the bass.

RESERVOIR SECTIONS

To simplify his search for largemouths on big reservoirs, Clunn divides each impoundment into three sections: 1) lower, 2) middle, and 3) upper. He characterizes tributaries by their proximity to each section of the reservoir, and applies his seasonal knowledge to each section to assess its likelihood for holding catchable bass.

During their seasonal migrations, bass follow submerged structures in reservoirs.

Early Prespawn Period—Look for places that warm faster than the rest of the lake. These will be in protected creek arms on the northwestern side, where cold winds are blocked and sunshine heats the water. Coves not susceptible to runoff also are more stable and attractive to bass. A temperature gauge is a must at this time, because one creek may be 10°F warmer than another one nearby.

Spawn Period—Clunn avoids spawning bass. Instead, he looks at other reservoir areas, in Sections 2 and 3, for example, for bass that have already moved into creek arms and coves following the spawn or have not bedded yet.

Postspawn Period—Once offshore-oriented late-spawning bass are done, he must focus on tough-to-catch postspawn fish. "The problem with the Postspawn Period is that it's a transition period, and patterns are fleeting. Once you find bass, they can be caught but may move several hundred yards by tomorrow."

To make the best of the situation, Clunn returns to areas where bass spawned first, reasoning that the Postspawn Period will be nearly over and bass will be settling into more predictable summer patterns.

Summer Period—"Early summer often provides the best deep-water fishing of the year," Clunn says. He searches the lower section of the reservoir for nearshore humps, channel bends, ledges, underwater points, and deep weededges. The best areas in summer, he says, are rather close to spawning coves, offering feeding grounds to hungry bass that have completed the spawn.

Mid-to-late Summer—High water temperatures, often linked to reduced dissolved oxygen, can stagnate bass activity most of the day. Clunn combats these effects by looking first at upstream, Section 3 habitat, where flowing water

Seasonal Reservoir Sections & Patterns

In late fall, bass shift to sections 1 and 2 of tributary arms.

During early and midsummer, check main-lake structure in sections 1, 2, and 3.

In late summer, the upper end of section 3 may offer the best action due to current, abundant cover, and reduced water clarity.

dam

headwaters

During a wet spring, focus on section 1 and 2 of arms in reservoir sections 1 and 2.

In early fall, check section 3 of all tributary arms.

In a dry spring, check sections 2 and 3 in arms of reservoir sections 1,2, and 3.

In winter, vertical structure with access to deep water attracts bass. Focus on sections 1 and 2 in tributary arms in reservoir sections 1 and 2.

To eliminate unproductive water, Rick Clunn uses a system of seasonal location patterns. He divides a reservoir into smaller sections and concentrates on those appropriate for that season. The lower end of a reservoir (1) begins at the dam and extends upstream about one third of the way up the main body of the reservoir; the upstream third (3) includes headwater tributaries. Section (2) is intermediate.

The lower section generally has the deepest and clearest water, while the upper end is shallower and more stained. Recent rains affect the upper section first and more strongly. Clunn similarly divides tributary creek arms into three sections that generally follow the depth and clarity characteristics of the main body of the reservoir.

brings in fresh oxygen and current positions baitfish. Upstream reaches also offer stained water, which keeps bass shallower and more active.

Fall Period—Upstream areas (3) become magnets for baitfish and bass when waters start to cool. This triggers faster feeding by bass.

Winter Period—"In Central states and southeastern reservoirs, winter is harder on anglers than on bass," Clunn says. Shallow tactics become less useful when bass move deeper on vertical structures and out of shallow cover in small creek arms. In early winter, he looks for deeper, well-defined channels and tight turns, where bass often group up. In late winter he looks shallow again, because slightly warming surface water draws fish upward and encourages them to feed. "On sunny days in February, I've often caught loads of bass in just a foot or two of water," Clunn says. "From those first preliminary movements stem the first prespawn movements of early spring."

RESERVOIR AGE

New reservoirs offer unique conditions that almost always support strong largemouth bass populations. Newly flooded land yields nutrients that promote dense plankton blooms, which in turn feed fish. Flooded timber and brush provide cover and nutrients. Prolific preyfish populations (shad, sunfish), fueled by plankton blooms, provide ample food for largemouths in the first few years of impoundment.

After several years, bass populations stabilize, adjusting to life among competing predators and prey species, and to changing reservoir conditions as reservoirs mature. Eventually, reservoirs begin to silt in. Their basins grow shallower, the pH shifts toward an extreme, and life becomes harder for all their inhabitants. As the bottom silts in, structure changes from its original flooded condition, and fertility often declines as well. Bass adapt to such changes, and so must the angler.

BASS BEHAVIOR IN RESERVOIRS

Like the studies that demonstrated hydrilla's role in rejuvenating Sam Rayburn Reservoir, John Hope's telemetry research on giant female largemouths in Texas reservoirs documents patterns critical to understanding bass location.

Briefly, what Hope discovered by tracking big bass was that from the Postspawn Period until fall, they were typically inactive and

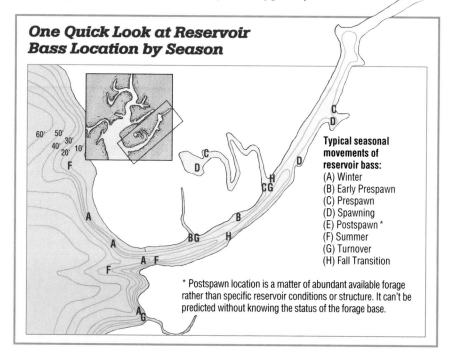

One Quick Look at Reservoir Bass Location by Season

Typical seasonal movements of reservoir bass:
(A) Winter
(B) Early Prespawn
(C) Prespawn
(D) Spawning
(E) Postspawn *
(F) Summer
(G) Turnover
(H) Fall Transition

* Postspawn location is a matter of abundant available forage rather than specific reservoir conditions or structure. It can't be predicted without knowing the status of the forage base.

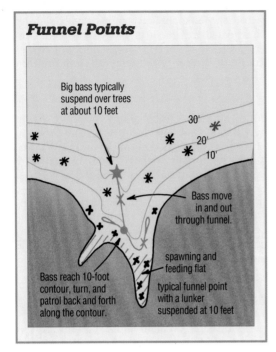

Funnel Points

Big bass typically suspend over trees at about 10 feet

30'
20'
10'

Bass move in and out through funnel.

Bass reach 10-foot contour, turn, and patrol back and forth along the contour.

spawning and feeding flat

typical funnel point with a lunker suspended at 10 feet

uncatchable all day long, holding outside the weededge not far from their spawning sites. Each evening, about an hour before nightfall, they moved away from these sites and swam toward shore, until they reached a 10- or 12-foot contour. There, they turned and swam parallel to the shore at a steady 1 mph, apparently trying to flush prey from cover. Just before dawn, they turned away from the break and swam back to their homes outside the weededge. In the cold months of the year, these fish fed during two distinct periods, each lasting about five hours: One began an hour after sunset, the other an hour before dawn.

Hope learned that in Sam Rayburn, big bass hold close to flats that offer the best spawning and feeding opportunities. They don't move far from these sites unless they're forced to by changing water-levels, lack of prey, or poor water-quality. They swim directly between these homes and their feeding grounds, not necessarily following cover or structure.

Ten feet appears to be the optimal depth for big bass in Texas reservoirs, apparently because this is the deepest a large bass can live and still easily swim to the surface to feed. Ten-foot breaklines around spawning and feeding shallows are these largemouths' favorite locations at night and during the hour and a half around dawn and dusk. He calls the areas where these fish move in and out from the breakline, "funnel points." Bass move through them on their daily patrol routes: they're the highest-percentage locations for hooking giant bass.

Hope's conclusions generally agree with those conducted by trackers on other impoundments. Bass tend to hold at constant depths, though these differ from reservoir to reservoir. This behavior is thought to be related to the largemouth's need to maintain its gas bladder at a constant pressure. Other researchers have found that smaller bass often hold in deeper water than the jumbo fish of Sam Rayburn. Possibly, larger fish like Hope's female lunkers must restrict their vertical movement because their gas bladders become proportionally weaker as their bodies grow larger. Larger fish in all studies were unlikely to feed during the day, when fishing pressure is high. They were most vulnerable when they moved shallow around the Spawn Period.

Tracking studies point to a conclusion you can bank on: The behavior of largemouths in reservoirs is consistent, if only for that particular body of water. Learn the routines of fish on your impoundment, and you'll know where to locate them.

Natural
Lakes

**CLASSIFYING
WATERS**

L imnologists have identified 11 different means of lake formation, many associated with glacial events of the last 17,000 years. About that time, vast glaciers formed during the last major ice age, the Wisconsin ice age. At its maximum, glaciers covered almost 32 percent of the earth's land area, compared to less than 10 percent today.

As the ice sheets of the late Pleistocene epoch receded, they left the Northern Hemisphere well endowed with lakes. Heavy rains over thousands of years filled the lakes and formed rivers as they drained to the north and south. Moving glaciers carried rocky material of all sizes and deposited it as ice melted, leaving huge boulders, along with hills and valleys.

Glacial Coverage

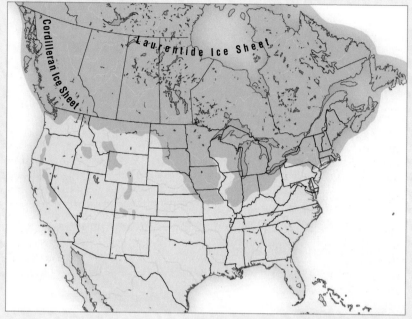

Map of southward glacial advancement during the Wisconsin Age. As they retreated, glaciers left behind the vast majority of our natural lakes. At the turn of the century, all inland fishing—except in Florida and a few other isolated regions—was restricted to either lakes in the areas formerly covered by glaciers or in rivers, streams, ponds, and backwaters.

Other lakes have formed from volcanic eruptions, earthquakes, uplifting and faults in geologic formations, landslides, changes in river channels (such as oxbow lakes), and impacts from extraterrestrial objects like meteors.

Whatever their source, the concave nature of lake basins inevitably leads to accumulation of sediments that results in the eventual death of a lake. Some lakes are by nature shortlived, while others would require millions of years to fill. Today, natural lake aging has been greatly enhanced by human activities that have encouraged siltation and nutrification, leading to premature lake aging.

These days, some of North America's most popular bassing waters are on large reservoirs in regions that lack natural lakes. Nevertheless, natural lakes should be part of your bassing experience, if only because this is where American bassing began.

THE AGE FACTOR

Natural lakes can generally be classified into one of three groups by age: young (oligotrophic), middle-aged (mesotrophic), and old (eutrophic). Along with such factors as prey base, aquatic vegetation, and shoreline development, lake age helps to determine where bass are likely to be located within any given Calendar Period.

All lakes change over time. Their first stage may last for millenia; their final one may occur quickly, particularly because of human activities. Natural lakes grow older not only in time but in condition. As lakes age, their bottom, depth, grade of drop-offs, vegetation, volume, oxygen content, pH, and other factors change. With these changes in habitat, the ratio, even the constitution, of fish species also shifts.

Because man-made changes on most North American lakes are the most significant source of lake aging, we classify natural lakes by their environmental condition rather than by their chronological age. Cultural eutrophication, or aging, is caused by farming practices, pollution, lake development, and other activities.

OLIGOTROPHIC LAKES

Environmentally young lakes are deep and clear, oxygen-rich, and rocky bottomed. They may support lake trout, whitefish, walleyes, and sometimes smallmouth bass. Such lakes are found almost exclusively in northern latitudes. They usually have steep, sharp drop-offs, deep basins, few weeds, large boulders, and shorelines rimmed by conifers. Nutrient levels are low and oxygen levels are high, even in deep water. Such waters are typically crystal clear. Smallmouth bass are more common in such lakes, although largemouths can be found in shallow, productive bays of some. Bass in these waters tend to grow slowly but may live for more than 15 years, so a few lunker-sized fish are possible. Oligotrophic lakes with good nutrient inputs may support larger populations of largemouths.

MESOTROPHIC LAKES

Middle-aged (mesotrophic) lakes are the most common type found from coast to coast at temperate latitudes. These lakes receive more nutrients from shoreline sources (originally rich stands of hardwoods) than do oligotrophic lakes; their shoreline terrain is more varied and their aquatic plants more diverse. The lakes themselves have more gradual drop-offs and smaller rocks; sand and gravel are more prevalent. Weedgrowth abounds on shallower flats. Such lakes are moderately fertile and support populations of many fish species. Many of the top largemouth lakes of the north-central, northwest, and northeast regions fall into this category.

NATURAL LAKE TYPES AND SELECT FISH SPECIES								
OLIGOTROPHIC			MESOTROPHIC			EUTROPHIC		
EARLY	MIDDLE	LATE	EARLY	MIDDLE	LATE	EARLY	MIDDLE	LATE
CONDITIONS OF ENVIRONMENT								
COLD WATER		TRANSITION STAGES		COOL WATER		TRANSITION STAGES		WARM WATER

LAKE TROUT

BULLHEAD

WALLEYE

LARGEMOUTH BASS

CATFISH

Middle–Stage Oligotrophic

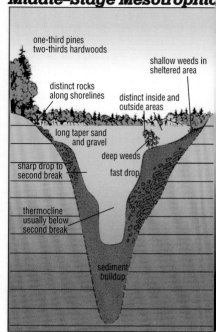

exposed lichen ledge
outcropping

spruce and pine trees
and a few white birches

few shallow weeds

steep
drop-offs

glacial rocks

occasional
tapering drop-offs

collapsed
sheets of rock

thermocline

oxygen
depletion
occurs at
deepest
depths

lake basin in
original ledge rock

sediment buildup

Depth in Feet
0
10
20
30
40
50
60
70
80
90
100
110

YOUNG

Middle–Stage Mesotrophic

one-third pines
two-thirds hardwoods

shallow weeds in
sheltered area

distinct rocks
along shorelines

distinct inside and
outside areas

long taper sand
and gravel

deep weeds

sharp drop to
second break

fast drop

thermocline
usually below
second break

sediment
buildup

MIDDLE-AGED

Middle–Stage Eutrophic

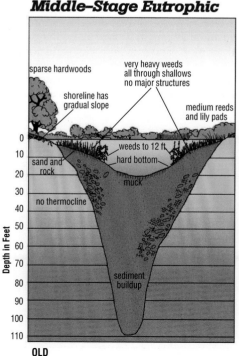

sparse hardwoods

very heavy weeds
all through shallows
no major structures

shoreline has
gradual slope

medium reeds
and lily pads

weeds to 12 ft

sand and
rock

hard bottom

muck

no thermocline

sediment
buildup

Depth in Feet
0
10
20
30
40
50
60
70
80
90
100
110

OLD

The Aging Processes

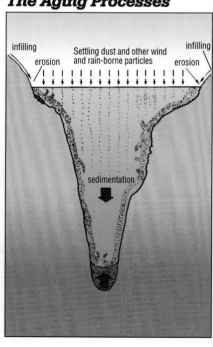

infilling

erosion

Settling dust and other wind
and rain-borne particles

infilling

erosion

sedimentation

EUTROPHIC LAKES

North America's oldest natural lakes are warmwater environments, generally shallow and rich in nutrients. Shallow weedgrowth remains thick as long as water stays fairly clear. Lake bottom consists of muck or clay deposited over millenia; shorelines taper gradually to waterlines. Such lakes often have no secondary drop-offs. Marshy areas often abut lake edges. Hardwood trees and flat shorelines are the rule.

Some eutrophic lakes are called "dishpan" lakes because of their uniformly shallow depth and shape. Oxbow lakes also fit this category. Typically, these old lakes have dense fish populations. Largemouths thrive in these rich, warm environments from Minnesota to Florida. In some late-stage eutrophic lakes, fish kills can occur because of oxygen depletion. When this happens, gamefish species like bass decline, ceding the waters to hardy bullheads, bowfin, gar, and carp.

These definitions also describe various kinds of artificial impoundments. The most significant difference lies in the constancy of water levels in natural lakes: Except during sustained droughts, natural lakes have more stable volumes and therefore more stable water temperatures and weedgrowth. And stability is what the largemouth seeks and thrives on.

THE IMPORTANCE OF VEGETATION

Field studies of bass behavior confirm that largemouths distribute themselves throughout the water column and in many habitats. Competition for space and food forces them into many areas that satisfy at least minimal habitat and food requirements. When largemouths need to feed under less than optimal conditions, they tend to drift along cover edges individually or in small aggregations, apparently hoping to approach unobserved within range of their prey, a ploy called the "habituation tactic." When conditions are more favorable and other hungry bass of similar size are nearby, largemouths tend to form loose schools and to hunt by swimming more actively, taking advantage of prey startled and flushed from cover. Studies demonstrate that adult bass attack successfully more than 70 percent of the time. Large fish have even higher success rates. When prey-fish are dense and bass aggregations are substantial, largemouths follow schooled prey into open water, darting near balls of bait and feeding on any isolated fish.

SPRING

The natural lakes most likely to harbor strong largemouth populations have luxuriant weedgrowth. Even in the North in early spring, bass depend on vegetation, growing or dead. In the shallow, black-bottomed bays that bass favor in early spring after ice-out, dried grasses scattered along the edges remain from the previous season. Clumps of grass with open pockets among and behind them are ideal. Old dead grass matted on the surface offers an early-season equivalent of weedgrowth. Lily pads are another key vegetation, both the trunk-like rhizomes that can be found on the bottom and floating, and new pads just unfurling.

When ice thins in early spring on northern lakes, it pulls big patches of mucky bottom toward the surface. Swamp gas is released, floating these patches. Bass swim in and out of holes in such floating masses, which warm fast because of their black surface. These are can't-miss locales for early-season bass on northern natural lakes.

On developed lakes, piers, boat docks and canals can concentrate bass, particularly when they're located toward the back end of bays. Brushpiles, blow-downs, pipes, and overhanging trees are also prime locations for early-season bass.

Ice–Out Hot Spots in Natural Lakes

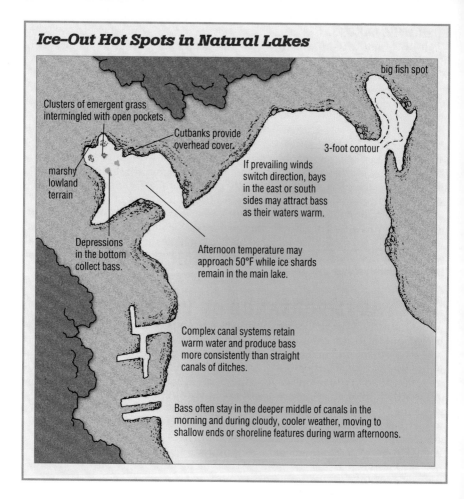

big fish spot

Clusters of emergent grass intermingled with open pockets.

Cutbanks provide overhead cover.

3-foot contour

marshy lowland terrain

If prevailing winds switch direction, bays in the east or south sides may attract bass as their waters warm.

Depressions in the bottom collect bass.

Afternoon temperature may approach 50°F while ice shards remain in the main lake.

Complex canal systems retain warm water and produce bass more consistently than straight canals of ditches.

Bass often stay in the deeper middle of canals in the morning and during cloudy, cooler weather, moving to shallow ends or shoreline features during warm afternoons.

Don't pass up cutbanks, formed when sections of bog float against more solid shoreline, providing extended canopies for bass. The ceilings of such cutbanks are held together by the roots of marsh grasses like cattails. On warm days, largemouths move to the edges of such structure or suspend near the surface. When days are colder, they pull beneath them, becoming impossible to reach.

Largemouths move directly to the back of canals in natural lakes in early spring. Protected from the wind, canals may be 12 degrees warmer than the open lake nearby. But if the wind pushes lake water into a canal, bass leave, entering another one whose entrance faces a different direction that insulates them from cold water.

After spawning, female largemouths in natural lakes gradually move off spawning flats while the males remain shallow, guarding eggs and fry. The key is locating secondary breaks outside of spawning areas, where bottom drops from about 5 to 12 feet. Females seem to funnel off the flats and hold temporarily along tight inside turns with rather fast breaks. If these breaks also have tiny fingers or small points, all the better. Note that females sometimes linger for days near nesting sites, even sitting on beds with the male.

After the spawn, females group on little corners, and newly growing vegetation acts as a bass magnet. Also look for breaks outside isolated spawning bays or backwater lakes, as bass hold there, too. Slight current flowing from such spots attracts sunfish, perch, shiners, and other preyfish.

Also look for changes in vegetation type, which signal edges that may hold bass: Coontail, pondweeds, and other submergent weeds grow in clumps from near bottom to the surface. Eurasian milfoil, on the other hand, tends to mat on the surface, allowing more open space in the water below. Offshore humps near spawning bays and flats also attract bass after the spawn. Those that rise to about 6 to 8 feet on top and contain a mixture of weeds and rock along the slopes seem best during the Postspawn Period. Look for largemouths along breaks that drop quickly to about 15 to 20 feet. Some big females also suspend between the shoreline break and humps and may relate to underwater points off humps.

In northern lakes in spring, largemouth females typically linger in shallow bays as long as they contain ripe eggs and males remain active. Once spawned out, females shift to areas with greater depth, more cover, and more preyfish. In many natural lakes, however, shallow bays are located off large embayments reaching depths of 15 feet or so. But the basins taper gradually, with slight rises and dips. Bays of this sort develop distinct weedlines that hold localized populations of bluegills, crappies, bullheads, shiners, and crayfish. Huge numbers of largemouths may remain in such spots for weeks, some lingering for months after the spawn.

The postspawn progression on natural lakes follows depth contours, with females and males that have completed their parental duties moving to 4- to 6-foot flats, where they hold near emerging weedbeds, sunken logs, boulders, and other objects that offer security.

As the waters warm toward summer, aquatic vegetation advances, choking some shallow areas and clearing the water. Largemouths then retreat deeper into weed clumps.

SUMMER

Many species of aquatic plants ring the clear natural lakes of the Northeast, the Northwest, the North-Central region, and Florida during summer, offering largemouths a variety of prime habitats. Look for breaks in the weedline, pockets and inside turns, and points where vegetation grows out along underwater extensions. Weededges along offshore humps also provide prime habitats for largemouths in summer. Open pockets within weedbeds sometimes occur when deeper holes or hard bottom breaks up otherwise uniform terrain. The surrounding weededges are bass magnets—and edges-within-edges can yield excellent catches.

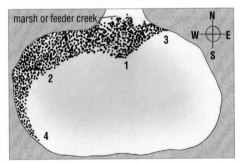

Overhead Cover (Lily Pads) in a Small Lake

marsh or feeder creek

Bass location in order of preference:
1. Pads run out deeper at the north end of the lake because the mouth of the creek forms a delta and the water is warmer here in spring.
2. The pad edge makes an inside turn.
3. & 4. Pads thin and disappear, indicating a change in bottom content and an attractive edge.

As soon as water warms toward 70°F in spring, masses of 'angel hair' filamentous algae may appear, particularly in lakes receiving excessive nutrients. This slimy stuff grows in pods that float on the surface or in midwater. It's usually found in quiet bays where wind doesn't disturb its development. Sometimes it grows among lily-pad fields, further enhancing their attraction to bass. Big bass love it, relating to this algae as long as it persists, which may be most of the summer in small fertile lakes.

By midsummer, many shallow lakes become dense with vegetation, and the best fishing usually appears in lily-pad fields where bass have room to roam. Some lily-pad roots are over 40 feet long, with hundreds of associated stalks. Bass usually hold right under the pads. Similarly, patches of duckweed at the mouths of coves are good bets for big bites when bass are active.

FALL

Fall anglers have some of the finest angling for big fish in the weeks after turnover, even when water temperatures drop below the 50°F range.

On natural lakes, cooling water causes a quick decline in thick submerged weedgrowth. Some plant species, like pondweed and cabbage, begin to dwindle long before the first frost. Milfoil and hydrilla, too, turn brown and apparently become less hospitable to bass. As these plants decompose, they free phosphorus, fueling plankton blooms and darkening the water. These changes shade the remaining green weeds and speed their senescence, shifting bass shallower so that they can see better.

Frosty nights thin the shallow weedgrowth and algae that have harbored shallow bass all summer. Water temperatures in the shallows may fluctuate by 5 to 8 degrees from morning to sunny afternoon.

At this time of year, inside turns on large flats tend to conserve their weedbeds best, and these areas with lush living cover attract bass and other species that evacuate points, humps, and other windblown structures, as well as shallow flats. The curve of inside turns fosters thick plant growth, as silt and organic materials are funneled off flats by wind and current and deposited here. This sheltering shape also protects weedbeds from wind and current.

Brett Richardson

Bass anglers look forward to fall fishing, as big fish feed heavily to store energy for winter, while thinning cover makes them easier to locate.

Check contour maps to locate desirable spots. Weedgrowth should be assessed visually and with sonar to determine if it holds fish. Choose corners on the leeward side of the lake or bay, or inside points that block the wind. In fall, largemouths seem more willing to bite in calm water.

WINTER

Most top largemouth lakes contain extensive vegetation, and its position and condition strongly affect bass location in late fall. As winter approaches, largemouths gather near the deep edge of weedbeds that remain alive and green. The greenest clumps typically grow along steep inside turns of shoreline breaks and on inside points of all sizes.

Vegetation depth varies with water clarity and substrate, but in winter, deeper is better. Look for outside edges in water from 9 to 20 feet deep. Substantial clumps of coontail and northern milfoil remain through early winter along deep breaks. Note, though, that the best spots are near shelves or flats on top of the breaks. They do not need to be large. In murkier lakes, vegetation is limited to shallower areas—perhaps 7 to 9 feet at the outside edge. Fertile lakes with dense algae blooms in summer often become quite clear after fall turnover. Plant growth can be sustained in such lakes, and largemouths occupy the best clumps along vertical breaks.

In lakes with little vegetation, steep rock slides and bouldered bluffs hold bass. Lacking rock, largemouths will hold along shorelines with steep slopes. Steep, narrow channels are prime wintertime bass spots, as they offer protection on both sides. To escape wind-generated currents, fish only have to swim a few hundred yards to the opposite bank. Such areas allow them to move easily to more sun-baked banks while remaining close to vertical structure.

In the North, December brings early-ice conditions. Underwater cameras lowered under the ice demonstrate that bass in winter are far from the lethargic creatures described in some popular and scientific reports, even though the water has descended into the mid-30°F range. Often a large bass will approach the camera lens and peer into it, like an apartment dweller looking out of a peephole to see who's ringing the bell. But they aren't much interested in feeding. They can be caught, but mostly when they're concentrated along a deeper break, where dozens of fish may occupy a room-sized spot.

A few hundred miles to the south and along the Atlantic Coast, winter largemouths in small natural lakes typically bite faster. And in the South, where largemouths spawn as early as December in south Florida's natural lakes, the peak for catching 10-pounders is December through February. In the central part of the state, the peak starts about a month later, from January through March, while in northern Florida, it's from February through April. The peak vulnerability of these big Florida bass occurs as spawn approaches and during the bedding phase, when the fish remain in shallow cover near their nest sites. Of course, it doesn't hurt that Florida's late-stage lakes are also very fertile and that their fish are genetically capable of growing large.

No matter where you live and fish, largemouths in natural lakes are likely to grow to impressive size, due to the constancy of water level, vegetation, oxygen level, and prey such bodies of water offer.

Chapter 9

Small Waters, Big Bass

Mike Blair

Ponds

**MANAGEMENT
AND MORE**

Chances are good that you learned to fish on one of North America's ponds—those modest, mostly approachable places built to water livestock, irrigate farmland, drive a millwheel, or provide waterfowl with nesting and rearing habitat. The fact that you may have long since given up pond fishing for bigger waters shouldn't deter you from reconnecting with these places, because statistically, your best chance of catching a 6-pound largemouth is on the most productive pond in your neighborhood.

Ponds are usually defined as human-made impoundments of fewer than 50 acres, though some are considerably larger. The first ponds were built by damming streams in the northeastern states and provinces to create hydropower. The East Coast is still full of aged millponds, many of which continue to offer surprisingly good fishing. Pond building boomed elsewhere in the U.S. during the Depression, when the U.S. Agricultural Conservation Program subsidized farmers who were willing to dig them. In 1934, just before the program began,

Types of Ponds

Important aspects of a pond are determined by its watershed, soil type, and size. Nearly all small waters that qualify as ponds fit one of four categories; most are one of three types of farm ponds—dug pond, built pond, and dammed creek—managed primarily for fishing.

Dug Pond—Farm ponds with shallow, featureless basins often are dug with earth-moving equipment. Runoff usually keeps them full, but supplemental pumping may be necessary during dry periods. Most are round or squared off.

Dug ponds generally are less than 5 acres, but good management can make them productive. Regular fertilization can keep them green with phytoplankton, fueling the food web and shading aquatic plants that can harm balance in small waters.

From spring through mid-fall, active bass roam the banks, provided the edge quickly drops into 2 or more feet of water. Casting parallel to the bank from shore usually works better than casting into the featureless depths. Of course, fallen trees, docks, stands of cattails or submerged weedbeds provide cover and feeding spots for bass. Overhanging trees hold fish, too. Bugs fall off the branches and sunfish gather to sip them. Bass lurk in the shadows to seize the occasional bluegill.

In many ponds of this type, phytoplankton photosynthesize and raise oxygen levels in surface waters during late morning and afternoon, particularly on sunny days. Oxygen levels decline with depth, often nearing zero on the bottom. This profile forces fish to suspend, and deep cranking bottom-bumping with worms can be fruitless. If water is pumped into a pond to restore the water level or to enhance oxygen levels, preyfish and bass move toward the flow.

Built Pond—An earthen dam across a low area can create a pond of up to 100 acres or so, as the dam backs up runoff water. The area near the dam is deepest, providing predictable wintering locations. The shallower upper end attracts fish in spring, as this area warms first and often offers more cover and structural features. Land and other features like underwater points and cuts hold fish. This type of pond functions as a miniature reservoir.

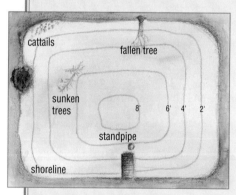

cattails
fallen tree
sunken trees
8' 6' 4' 2'
standpipe
shoreline

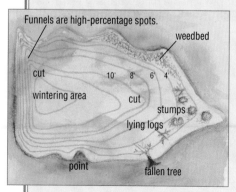

Funnels are high-percentage spots.
weedbed
cut
10' 8' 6' 4'
wintering area
cut
stumps
lying logs
point
fallen tree

Dammed Creek—Small creeks are dammed for irrigation and fishing. Those dammed for power production generally produce impoundments larger than what we're calling ponds. The creek channel and any feeder channels are focal points for bass location during all seasons. Standing timber and stumps on points or channel turns hold bass during all seasons, except during the spawn.

If current from the creek is substantial, the pond won't stratify thermally or chemically (such as the oxycline often found in dug and built ponds). Some bass may move onto deep structure in summer, while others remain in shallow cover. Ponds of this type usually are large, sometimes surpassing 100 acres. Successful fishing patterns diversify with pond size.

Most dammed creeks aren't managed as intensively as small farm ponds because of the expense and labor. Weedbeds and wild fish such as shiners, bullheads, pickerel, and other non-stocked species complicate the bass-bluegill balance, but waters

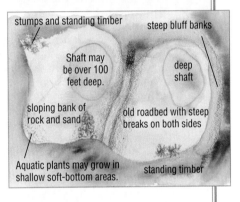

of this type can produce huge bass, particularly if fishing pressure on bass is light. In some regions, ponds of this type are open to anglers who drop a buck or two in a can nailed to a fence post. "Dollar ponds," they're called in south Georgia. Hawg bass await skilled bass hunters or lucky novices.

Pits—In mining areas, pits often fill with rainwater or spring water when mining operations cease. Some mines have been reclaimed for recreation. Those under 100 acres technically qualify as ponds, though their characteristics differ greatly from classic farm ponds. Where water chemistry is suitable (exclude coal mines), bass, bluegills, catfish, and wild species thrive.

Pits are typically deep and clear, so their productivity varies with shape, preyfish, and productivity. When harvest is limited, some Florida phosphate pits produce extraordinary bass fishing due to their high fertility. Shallow pits are typically more productive than deep pits.

Highway construction often requires major excavation, leaving broad, shallow holes that eventually fill with water and fish. Managers can formulate a fish stocking plan to produce the best fishing, though public access to these spots can confound the best plans.

Average Largemouth Bass Growth in Ponds

State	Age (years)							
	1	2	3	4	5	6	7	8
Illinois	6	9	12	14	16	17	20	
Southern Indiana	4.5	8	11.5	14	16	18		
Northern Indiana	3	6.5	9.5	12	14	16		
Iowa	10	12	13.5	15	16.5			
Kansas	9	11	13	15	16.5			
South Dakota	4	7	10	12	14	16	17	18

the U.S. had an estimated 20,000 ponds. By 1965, there were more than 2 million. Today, there are probably 3 million ponds in the U.S., the majority in what is known as the "pond belt"—a band of states stretching from northern Virginia to southern Montana and the regions south of that line—in which about 1,000 new ponds are built each year.

Even the smallest of these—under 10 acres—provide more than 100 million fishing days every year for an estimated 9.9 million anglers. In states that keep close tabs on pond fishing, a sizable proportion of all fishing occurs on ponds: In Kansas, for example, more than 24 percent of all fishing days by licensed anglers are spent on ponds. In North Carolina, 19 percent of licensed anglers fish ponds more frequently than rivers, lakes, or reservoirs; in Georgia, that figure is 42 percent. Each year, more people fish ponds than any other kind of water. And we suspect even more anglers would focus on them if they knew what spectacular fishing well-managed ponds can provide.

Of course, most ponds do not harbor 6-pound lunker bass and one-pound bluegills (bream) just waiting for you to drop your line in front of them. Unfortunately, at least 75 percent of ponds are not managed properly or have become ecologically imbalanced. And because their ecosystems are small and basically artificial, ponds suffer disproportionately when they're neglected. It was probably catching countless stunted bluegills or thin, runty bass one too many times that prompted you to look to larger waters in the first place. So the basic rule of pond fishing is this: Learn to read ponds accurately. You'll need to understand predator-prey balance, selective harvest, largemouth locations by season, and pond management—or mismanagement.

PREDATOR-PREY BALANCE

Whatever the region, largemouth bass drive the dynamics of pond life. They can thrive in small waters and grow to maximum size there. The key to understanding whether or not a pond is likely to support big ones is to understand their balance with bluegills, their usual prey. When the two species are in balance, fishing can seem incredible for anyone accustomed to slower fishing in natural lakes or big reservoirs.

The primary cause of imbalance in ponds is overharvest of bass. Without enough bass to keep them controlled, bluegills reproduce excessively. Overcrowding causes competition for food among them, which slows their growth. The resulting droves of 2- to 5-inch fish consume all the zooplankton in the pond. Such overcrowding can inhibit the spawning of both bluegills and bass.

The key to maintaining predator-prey balance is what we call selective harvest: Ensuring that there are enough bluegills to feed the bass and that enough bass remain in the system to control bluegill populations. Several factors may contribute to imbalances, including poor pond design and fishkills. But the most important factor is how many large bass remain in the pond system. The key to that is the critical management tool that lies with anglers, and their use, or misuse, of selective harvest.

SELECTIVE HARVEST

This is the key to maintaining balance in a pond. By selective harvest, we mean harvesting fish of certain sizes and species from an aquatic system in order to further management goals—in this case, growing big largemouths (in other cases, large bluegills).

In unfertilized ponds in the Southeast, biologists recommend annual harvesting of up to 10 pounds of bass per acre and up to 65 pounds of bluegills. In fertilized ponds, twice these amounts may be harvested. At a minimum, about 6 pounds of bluegills should be removed for every pound of bass. In such fertile, warm waters, some largemouth females may reach 9 pounds within six years of stocking. Many bluegills will exceed one pound, and redears may grow even larger.

In northern ponds, largemouths are so easy to catch that biologists from Kansas, Missouri, and states to their north hesitate to specify how many pounds of bass should be removed from a balanced pond each year. Overharvest can easily occur when bass have spawned poorly during one or more springs. In a pond's fifth post-stocking year, one recommendation is to harvest thirty 8- to 12-inch bass per acre and none that are 12 to 15 inches. Larger bass can be harvested as well. If the pond's manager is aiming for big bass, all large fish should be released. Particularly on small ponds, catch and release of bass is critical to sustaining superior fishing.

Keeping an abundant population of adult bass in a pond reduces the density of bluegills and accelerates their growth rate. The result may be fewer bluegills, but those that remain will be larger. In southern ponds managed for big sunfish, where many bluegill and redear exceed 10 inches, managers limit removal of bass per acre per year to fewer than 5 pounds. In the North, high-density largemouth populations can also increase the size of crappie and yellow perch populations to trophy sizes.

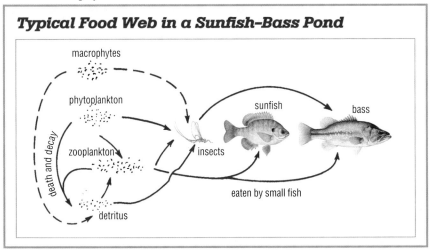

Typical Food Web in a Sunfish–Bass Pond

macrophytes

phytoplankton

zooplankton

death and decay

detritus

insects

sunfish

bass

eaten by small fish

POND LOCATIONS BY SEASON

Ponds are delicate systems, particularly when they first fill. Typically, they are scooped out of fertile farmland by a bulldozer or created by damming a small creek to fill a natural depression. In both cases, run-off from surrounding croplands stains the pond in spring and after big summer or fall rains. Summer drought can draw down the pond to well below its weedline, concentrating its fish and altering its composition. Far more so than a natural lake or a reservoir, a pond can vary radically in level from season to season and year to year.

Most ponds contain a mixture of fish species. Typically, they are stocked with largemouths, bluegills, and channel catfish. Other species—carp, bullheads, shiners, crappies, and other sunfish—may be introduced through flooding or unintentional stockings (for example, by an angler who releases remaining baitfish into the pond). Such stockings are always undesirable.

One of the chief differences between pond and reservoir fishing for bass is that with ponds, you know the fish are in there—the only question is exactly where. You're fishing in 15 feet of water or less most of the time. Everything's miniaturized—except (if you're lucky) the fish.

Factors that determine where largemouths and their prey can be found in larger bodies of water apply to ponds, too. Like their cousins in reservoirs and natural lakes, largemouths in ponds thrive in clear to moderately stained water with moderate amounts of vegetative cover. Creek channels, points, flooded trees, stumpfields, weedbeds, weedy or brushy shoreline, overhanging willows, and cattails attract and hold bass, just as they do on bigger waters.

Spring—In early spring, ponds warm much faster than bigger bodies of water. Small bays or channels on their north sides attract largemouths when water temperatures rise. Bass nose into the shallows to warm themselves and to feed on smaller fish that are searching for insects and zooplankton. Look for weedy areas near drop-offs, because bass use deeper breaks to travel from one shallow spot to another.

It's hard to go too shallow in a pond during spring; largemouths regularly venture into water less than a foot deep. Even though weeds haven't developed much by early spring, bass can be located around the previous year's weedline. Their best cover at this time of year consists of stumps, rocks, brown bulrushes, and other semi-permanent or permanent features. They also patrol the edges of small creeks that pour into the pond, feeding on prey that washes in. Look for them, too, along the banks of most ponds, where shallow shelves drop off into deeper water. The degree of drop and the depth of water may be slight in shallow ponds or pronounced in deeper (20-foot) ones.

During the Prespawn and Spawn Periods, bass spend more time in the shallows and become more active while there. They're attracted to weedgrowth and to areas that collect heat because of dark rocks, sandy bottom, and bulrushes. The best shoreline cover will be near deep water in areas protected from wind.

Summer—Because ponds are typically small, they warm up (and cool off) much faster than larger bodies of water. During the Postspawn Period, largemouths in ponds change their habits. Now that the water is warm, they feed in the shallows only when the sun isn't beating down. Look for them in nearby deep water and watch for points, pockets, and lanes that concentrate bass. The first hours of daylight and the last hour before sunset become prime times on ponds, especially when it's hot. Vegetation is growing rapidly now, and bass

Pond Features

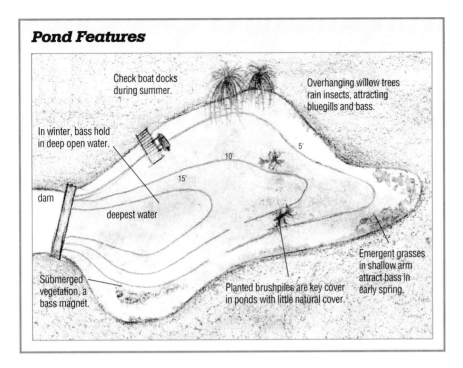

Check boat docks during summer.

Overhanging willow trees rain insects, attracting bluegills and bass.

In winter, bass hold in deep open water.

10'

5'

15'

dam

deepest water

Submerged vegetation, a bass magnet.

Planted brushpiles are key cover in ponds with little natural cover.

Emergent grasses in shallow arm attract bass in early spring.

use it for shade, ambushing prey, and resting. During extremely hot weather, the oxygen given off by weedbeds creates a more comfortable location for fish than deeper areas with little or no weedgrowth and low oxygen levels. If there's a light wind, it may extend action from cool morning into midday.

Night fishing is the key to pond action during summer. While some bass retreat to deeper water after dark, many return to the shallows to feed on sunfish and minnows.

Fall—In late summer and fall, largemouths tend to concentrate around the more distinctive parts of deeper weedlines, particularly the points and fingers along weededges. During unstable weather, they may move into inside bends or pockets within deeper weedlines. Inactive bass tend to group tightly and lie close to bottom.

Winter—In the North, winter can be a harsh time on shallow ponds. Fishkills are not uncommon. Shallower ponds can become oxygen-depleted so they cannot support life. Ice fishermen are familiar with these conditions; holes augured into such ponds will literally disgorge desperate fish jumping to the surface in search of oxygen. Very shallow ponds can freeze from top to bottom. Such events can alter predator-prey dynamics come the following spring, which is one of the reasons active management of ponds is often necessary.

POND MANAGEMENT

Assessing the likelihood of locating good-sized largemouths in a pond depends on knowing what the pond is managed for. Unlike large lakes and reservoirs, well-managed ponds are usually maintained only to benefit one or two species. The keystone species that interests us—the largemouth—is only part of a pond's story, only one of its important players.

In southeastern states, pond owners typically stock new or renovated ponds in fall with 500 fingerling bluegills per acre, or 1,000 fingerlings if the pond is fertilized. The following May or June, they add 50 fingerling bass per acre, or 100 per acre in fertilized waters. In this food-rich environment, bluegills grow fast and are ready to spawn after seven months or so in a new pond. The newly stocked fingerling bass eat the resulting bluegill fry and prevent overpopulation by the bream. Bluegills continue to spawn throughout summer, providing food for bass. By the age of one, largemouths should be ready to spawn. In turn, their offspring will eat that spring's newly hatched bluegills. This balanced cycle can now be maintained if selective harvest is applied. Some southern ponds are stocked with shiners or shad instead of bream or in addition to sunfish, and largemouths com-

Growing Trophy Bass

So you really want to catch trophy bass from your pond, say bass larger than 8 pounds? You can, with good management (selective harvest) and a little time, if the pond stays balanced. First, think about carrying capacity. If the pond only supports 30 pounds of bass per acre, you won't have many bass if they average 5 or 6 pounds.

The best way to grow trophy bass in a typical balanced pond is to use a slot limit. Initially, protect bass 14 to 18 inches long, harvesting bass smaller and larger than the protected size. After a couple years, increase the slot to 16 to 20 inches; again harvest bass smaller and larger than the protected size. After a couple more years, continue to harvest bass smaller than 16 inches and a few in the 16 to 20-inch slot.

Watch the condition of the bass; more harvest of certain sizes is needed if fish in that size group are in poor condition. At least annually, take seine samples to make sure the pond has young bass as well as small and intermediate-size sunfish. This approach will grow trophy bass while maintaining a diversity of sizes of bass necessary to keep the pond balanced.

Should you release a trophy fish so it can grow larger? Indeed, released fish can be and often are caught again. You don't, however, want a large portion of the pond's carrying capacity tied up in large bass that will die of old age. Generally, no harm is done by occasionally harvesting bass over 6 pounds. If you want to see if a particular bass is caught again, clip a pelvic fin (one of the paired fins on the belly behind the gill covers) or the first 2 or 3 spines of the dorsal fin.

Mike Blair

ing from such ponds have trophy potential. In some, an initial infusion of fathead minnows helps bass growth.

In northern ponds, stocking strategies differ. In South Dakota, for example, intermediate-sized bluegills are added to a pond the fall after bass were stocked in spring. Fathead minnows may be stocked along with the bluegills at a rate of about 3 pounds per acre. Because all species grow more slowly in the North, biol-

Ponds are the ideal place to introduce kids to fishing and demonstrate new techniques to novice anglers.

ogists recommend that no bass be harvested until four years after stocking. In Kansas, some ponds are stocked with gizzard shad as well as bluegills—a combination that produces big bass. (It also results in poor bluegill fishing, as shad compete with the 'gills.)

To determine what the prospects are for a particular pond, ask the owner if almost all of his bass get released. If they do, the pond is apt to contain lunkers. If the owner seems to harvest his bass instead, they have probably been reduced to a level at which they can't control the bluegills, and large fish will be scarce. Public ponds often suffer this fate because anglers who fish them tend to keep their catches. Be sure to ask the pond's manager if it's all right to keep any of your catch; he may want you to remove some as part of his management plan. Good managers often do.

What if you're fishing a pond about which you have no information—say, a pond on public land or on a back 40 you have access to?

If you find many small bass in an unknown pond, move on or else bring your panfish tackle: Chances are that the bluegills or redears will be large and that bass area overabundant and thus slow-growing and small. A few large old bass may be present. The combination of big bream and few small bass, on the other hand, suggests that big bass may be swimming around there, too, particularly if the pond is an old one.

The challenge of locating largemouths on these miniature waters never pales for many of North America's finest anglers. They know that ponds are the birthplace of bass fishing and that the best of them offer better bassing—more and bigger fish per hour—than the latest reservoir hot spots. Moreover, ponds offer the sort of slow, contemplative angling that attracted many of us to bass fishing in the first place. They're also an ideal place to introduce kids to fishing and demonstrate new techniques to novice anglers.

Rich Zaleski

Bass in Current

RIVERS, CREEKS, CULVERTS, AND DITCHES

I f you don't think of largemouth bass as river fish, consider this: Their distribution across eastern and central North America was made possible by migration through the continent's mighty river systems some tens of thousands of years ago.

After the retreat of Pleistocene glaciers, largemouths swam north and west from their homewaters in southeastern North America until they reached southern Canada and the Texas Gulf Coast. When glacial waters receded, many strains of bass were stranded in the enclosed basins we call lakes. We've been calling them lake fish ever since.

The warm and sluggish waters of the St. Johns River in Florida, or the waters of the lower Mississippi—rivers that were the largemouth's ancestral homes—offered cover and prey along weedy shores, oxbows, and sloughs—plenty of structure where fish could hold, deep holes for wintering, and sandy, firm bottoms for spawning. It's not surprising, then, that largemouths thrive in big warm rivers, including some in the West, where they were introduced in the nineteenth century. But that's hardly the end to the story of bass in current: Largemouths can also be found in smaller rivers, creeks, culverts, and ditches. And we're not talking little bass, either—8- and 9-pounders can be found in running waters. Now, how to find them?

THE NATURE OF CURRENT

It's almost a matter faith with bass anglers that largemouths avoid current. If you think about what currents offer bass, however, you'll see that moving water has a lot to recommend it.

Bass, we know, like stability in their environment—they expend less energy in locations that don't change much. It's true that lakes and reservoirs offer them stability on seasonal bases, but still waters fluctuate considerably in temperature, cover, oxygen level, and forage abundance from season to season. In the North and Central regions, lakes and reservoirs turn over in fall, freeze up in winter, and grow and lose much of their cover in between. By comparison, desirable stretches of river or creek offer largemouths more constant water temperatures, dissolved oxygen levels, and cover. And while small bass in current tend to wander, big bass often are homebodies. Telemetry studies demonstrate that most of them don't wander much farther than a few dozen feet from their seasonal lies. They find everything they need in or near current, and they grow big.

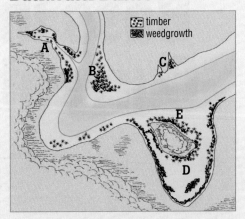

Backwater Basics

🔲 timber
🔲 weedgrowth

A

B

C

E

D

*Consistent fishing for largemouths in rivers rests with eliminating unsuitable areas. Largemouths need cover away from heavy current. The obvious largemouth holding spots in this river area include **Areas A, C,** and **D**. **Inside Bend Area B** may also attract fish because cover is present, and inside bends usually offer reduced current. Areas like **E** that are adjacent to good backwater areas should hold a few fish. As a rule, however, concentrate on areas away from main current.*

Besides the greater stability that some rivers offer, they offer the edge effect in abundance: The attraction that marked changes in habitat provide animals. The edge between swift and slow current attracts both large predators like bass and the smaller fish they prey on.

Let's look at the five primary factors that determine bass location in rivers: Dissolved oxygen, current, water temperature, cover, and baitfish.

DISSOLVED OXYGEN

In northern waters that freeze over, the most critical habitat for bass is one that contains enough dissolved oxygen. During winter, oxygen levels drop steadily in backwater channels; once they reach 2 parts per million (ppm), which often happens in late February, bass seek out better water. Winterkills of largemouths in backwaters have occurred when dissolved oxygen levels fell below 2 ppm throughout a large area.

Fishing River Bass

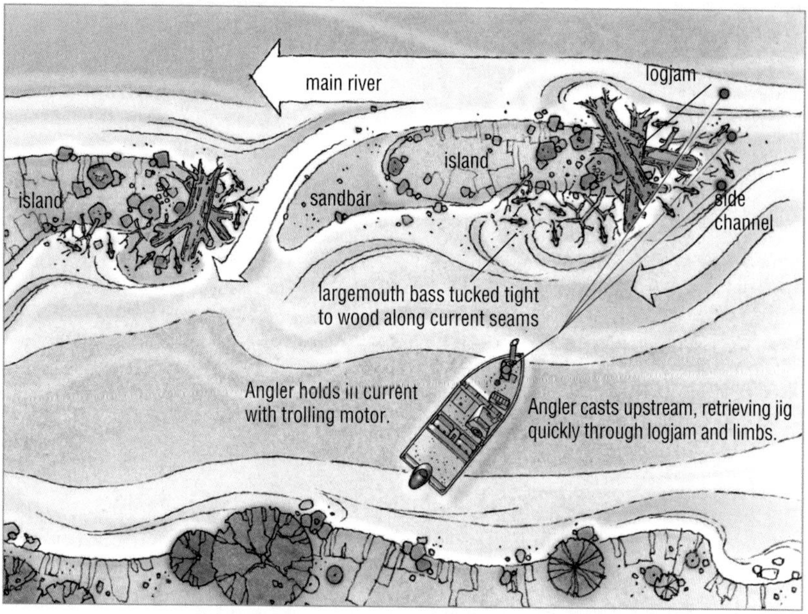

main river

logjam

island

island

sandbar

side channel

largemouth bass tucked tight to wood along current seams

Angler holds in current with trolling motor.

Angler casts upstream, retrieving jig quickly through logjam and limbs.

In such cases, bass typically move closer to current without actually moving into it. They don't seem to know where oxygen levels are higher, but they do instinctively seek deeper downstream spots. If oxygen levels aren't much higher there, they die. In a classic tracking study on the Mississippi River by Iowa DNR biologist John Pitlo, two tagged bass apparently succumbed to oxygen depletion. After ice-out, they were found along with several hundred other dead fish.

Overwintering spots with sufficient dissolved oxygen may be scarce in northern river systems and thus constitute a limiting factor on bass populations there. Pitlo's research, on a 15-mile stretch of the Mississippi River between Iowa and Illinois, revealed only three spots suitable for largemouths to overwinter. Farther south where waters don't freeze, river bass have more available spots to choose from. Even in such warmer waters, however, they are likely to move in winter from shallow oxbows and backwaters they inhabit in summer because of declining dissolved-oxygen levels. In other river systems, bass behavior in winter may vary, however (see Tracking Winter Bass sidebar).

During spring, river bass use diverse habitats. When spring floods inundate bottomland timber adjacent to riverbanks, bass readily enter this new habitat. During low water, they move into stumps, brush, or logs soon after ice-out. When floodwaters recede and weeds begin to grow, bass move into weedbeds and hold along weededges. Some bass may spawn near overwintering spots if suitable habitat is available. Others move miles to specific spawning locations. They remain there until early June, then move to summer areas.

Bass enter side channels and cuts that connect backwaters with the river, holding there until oxygen levels become too low in late summer and send them back to the main river. When summer's weeds decay under ice, they use up oxygen in

Tracking Winter Bass

Past tracking studies of river largemouth bass have suggested that fish congregate and overwinter in deep areas (10+ feet). Biologists with the Maryland Department of Natural Resources conducted a telemetry study on the tidal Chester River, following bass through fall and winter. One group of seven bass, tagged in Morgan Creek, a tributary, provided new insights into preferred winter habitat.

During fall, all seven stayed outside the mouth of Morgan Creek. When water temperatures fell further, five of the seven moved about three miles upstream into shallow headwater areas less than three feet deep, although deeper locations were available closer to their summer and fall locations.

The bass that moved upstream stayed in water as shallow as three feet at low tide, each in different locations. While some bass held near typical habitat like submerged trees and pilings, they were just as likely in the middle of the shallow creek, which was devoid of cover. This pattern continued throughout winter, even when the tributary was ice covered.

Warming temperatures in March stirred all the bass to move downstream, with five of the seven leaving Morgan Creek. The two that remained in the creek held in specific submerged trees from spring into the following fall.

Overwintering of largemouth bass in shallow headwater portions of tidal streams had not previously been reported, and this finding has important implications for resource management. In some areas, pier and breakwall construction is permitted in winter, when impacts on bass were thought to be minimal because of the belief that bass overwinter in deep holes. Our results suggest that this isn't always the case, and in-stream work might disturb fish during a period when they could not recoup energy losses.

This study also reinforces the fact that while our knowledge of bass behavior is increasing, there's still much we do not understand. Continued research on bass habitat and movement is vital to wise fishery management in the future.

Alan Heft
Maryland Dept. Nat. Res.

the process. If dissolved oxygen levels fall below 2 or 3 ppm, largemouths must find new places to hold until ice-out. They seek out the mouths of inflowing tributaries, culverts, and pipes, all of which offer more oxygenated or cooler water. In rivers, they move closer to current, where water holds more oxygen.

Come fall, river bass seem to get pushed out of the dying beds of submerged weeds by low dissolved-oxygen levels. Submerged weedbeds are abandoned first; some bass remain in the bare stalks until late fall, when they move into woody cover.

Pitlo's telemetry studies suggest that largemouth bass usually move into the upper end of their overwintering areas in December, just before ice-up. These seasonal shifts can involve long distances. For two consecutive years, one of Pitlo's bass moved nine river miles upstream from its summer location near a series of cuts to an overwintering slough out of the Mississippi's current. It bypassed two other spots used by other bass to overwinter.

CURRENT

Current delivers food and oxygen, but it also creates energy demands on fish. Largemouths avoid holding directly in the strongest current; you'll find them to the side of it or in pockets out of direct flow, like downstream of boulders, undercut banks, fallen timber, points, and stumps—anything that breaks up or lies adjacent to current.

For spawning, river bass seek spots that lack current. They may

Effects of Flow

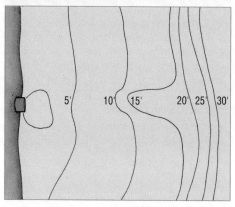

Especially on waters that undergo a sizable yearly drawdown, check for an erosion ditch at the outer edge of the flat, even if the depression near the pipe is silted in.

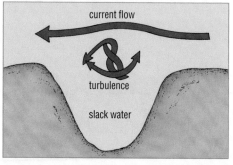

In rivers, gullies like this create an unseen current break substantial enough to hold huge groups of fish.

travel as far to find suitable areas for spawning as they do for suitable winter habitat. River largemouths typically spawn in 1- to 3-foot water over hardpan sand or clay covered by a few inches of silt.

Once spawning is over, river bass seek areas with thick cover and reduced current, often in backwaters or sloughs. There, they'll hold in water only a foot or two deep. In summer, big river largemouths, like their lake and reservoir counterparts, are homebodies. Once they find locations to their liking, they stay put except to feed.

Small creeks, particularly in the Southeast, often hold large bass. When those creeks have been dammed, current slows and forms pools that often provide perfect habitat for big largemouths. Even when current is slight, creek bass typically hold downstream from cover. When current increases because of rain, creek bass move to more protected areas. Their locations become highly predictable at such times, though feeding may be sporadic.

Tidal rivers offer an exceptional form of current. Along the Atlantic, Pacific, and Gulf coasts, they offer excellent bass fishing. Many tidal rivers and marshes are vast and receive less fishing pressure than nearby lakes and reservoirs. In general, bass in tidal systems don't live as long or grow as large as bass in still waters, yet they are notably strong and fight hard. In the California Delta, however, bass over 10 pounds are often caught. Twice a day at high tide, salty ocean water pushes inland, flooding associated marshes and pockets. The flow of incoming water can be strong enough to reverse the flow of tidal rivers. When the tide ebbs, marshes rapidly lose volume and may become too shallow for bass. Largemouths seem to have an instinctive concern about being caught in shallow water, moving downstream at ebb tides to avoid being trapped in isolated pools.

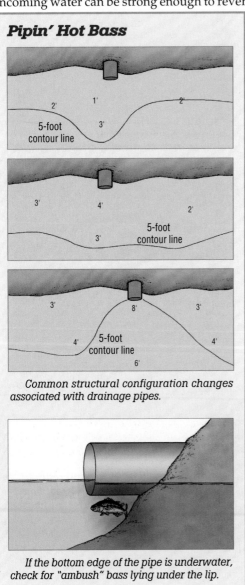

Pipin' Hot Bass

Common structural configuration changes associated with drainage pipes.

If the bottom edge of the pipe is underwater, check for "ambush" bass lying under the lip.

Drainage pipes and culverts aren't exactly rivers, but the water in them moves and it's invariably different from lake water—warmer, colder, dingier, clearer, richer. If it flows regularly, chances are that bottom beyond its mouth is scoured or otherwise different from bottom nearby. Such areas draw bass.

Pipes that dump fertilizer-rich runoff into otherwise low-fertility areas are another form of current that attracts bass. You can sometimes spot the lush aquatic vegetation that marks the outlet of a pipe even before you can see it. Fish are drawn not to the pipe but to the water conditions created by the run-off, drainage, or wastewater that spews out. Largemouths can be found on the outside edge of flats in front of drainage pipes on fluctuating flowages or on the upper reaches of impoundments or in rivers. Look for ditches or washed-out gullies when the flowage or impoundment is drawn down. Often, the depression near the mouth of a pipe is silted in or poorly defined, but the channel cut by its flow is visible closer to the breakline into the main channel. Such ditches are deeper than the flat and have sharp breaks. Under high or normal water conditions, they offer pockets of slack water because the river current flows across the top of them. These spots are a goldmine for bass in spring and summer.

Culverts are similar to drainage pipes, except that they're at least partially under water at all times and are usually open at both ends. Most anglers are interested in the waters lying beyond one end of a culvert, particularly if they can get their boat through it. But the culvert itself is worth checking out—it's an important breakline, a place where two different habitats meet. If potentially attractive bass habitat—say, riprap leading into 4 feet or more of open water—lies on one side of a causeway, and shallow, weedy backwater on the other, the first area to check is the dark culvert itself. It may be key.

Largemouths avoid holding directly in the strongest current; you'll find them to the side of it or in pockets out of direct flow.

The type of structure above a culvert can be a major factor in determining whether or not big bass lurk below. Culverts under back roads with little traffic are worth checking out. Tapering concrete walls that extend into the water on either side of a culvert to prevent soil from washing into its mouth function like points at the mouths of tributaries. Highway crossings on wide flatland and lowland reservoirs may function like causeways. In such places, the elevated bridge crosses the narrow channel of an old river. Culverts beneath may not be visible at normal water levels—the best ones aren't readily visible unless the lake is drawn down—but they usually pass through the causeway every few hundred yards. These spots turn on when water is drawn through the reservoir or when wind pushes water through them.

Whenever you spot a creek entry or substantial drainable ditch along the shoreline, take the time to check for submerged roadbeds running parallel to the shore—you're almost certain to find culverts beneath the roadbeds. These culverts offer unique bottom structure. They don't have to be deep to be productive.

WATER TEMPERATURE

Remember that stable habitat is the key to locating bass in streams. Places where springs or tributaries enter a river are most likely to offer constant year-round temperature and dissolved oxygen. Bass that live in such areas experience fewer environmental extremes and so tend to live longer and grow larger.

River largemouths are less active when water temperature drops below 50°F. But once the water approaches 60°F in spring, fishing can be excellent. Bass become active, catchable, and on the move—they're headed for spawning sites.

COVER

Like their still-water cousins, river bass depend on cover to ambush prey, to deflect energy-sapping current, and to avoid becoming prey, themselves.

After the Spawn Period, river largemouths migrate into summer feeding areas. In the fertile sloughs and backwaters they favor, duckweed, algae and lily pads often grow in thick mats, forming moving canopies of cover. Largemouths skulk beneath the duckweed, using ambush as a feeding tactic.

Not all river largemouths abandon main channels in summer, however. They can be found along pilings, navigation towers, wingdams, and shoreline eddies. Natural cover like boulders, holes near tributary mouths, and fallen trees host

Gord Pyzer

During summer, river largemouths fatten up on shad.

them, too. When trees fall into the stream flow, their trunk and branches serve as current breaks. Usually they rest with their root system upstream and their branches downstream, parallel to stream flow. Bass use the downstream side, often far out toward the ends of branches. They also hold and feed around river weeds: Arrowhead, pickerelweed, cabomba, lily pads, coontail, eelgrass, and pepper grass are popular summer cover.

In fall, weedstalks on the outside edge of expansive flats continue to hold largemouths until it's time to return to overwintering areas. Look for bass on the inside bends of weedlines in 4 to 10 feet of water. Even in cooler fall weather, lily pads and lotus can attract bass, so investigate these. Once weeds have receded, wood becomes cover-of-choice for fall bass. In the North, they return in stages to overwintering areas, arriving before ice-up, usually in late September to early October but sometimes as late as December. They may move 10 or more miles in some systems. Pitlo's fish were active for a few more weeks after migration, then settled into a small area just prior to ice-up. In southern rivers, bass remain more active into early winter. They seek deeper areas with no current after water temperatures drop below 50°F.

In small creeks, largemouths typically live in deep holes located at sharp outside bends. When these are enhanced by woodcover, they're even more attractive to bass. Where such holes aren't available, bass make use of stumps, boulders, snags, rockpiles, bridge abutments, cypress trees, and other objects that blunt the force of current. Largemouths lie tight to these, ready to seize food. Weed islands, particularly isolated ones, offer lunkers much-needed structure in small rivers. So do undercut banks, bridge pilings, and creek bends, where floating logs and trash accumulate. The fact is, small creeks don't offer largemouths many choices of location—if you spot suitable habitat on small moving waters, bass are likely to be there and to stay put. For this reason, they can be frequently found on stretches of small creeks flowing through housing developments, where water levels and cover are maintained for the benefit of people, also to the benefit of bass.

In tidal rivers, largemouths use emergent and submerged vegetation and current breaks like stumps, bridge abutments, and rocks as cover when they move downstream from marshes. They often hold in little holes or dips in marshes and tidal creeks. Mussel beds or other hard bottom areas also attract numbers of fish.

BAITFISH

Small creeks that hold big largemouths offer plentiful and varied forage: crayfish, sunfish, minnows, suckers, darters, and shad, as well as small reptiles, amphibians, and small mammals like mice. Some small rivers have a wider variety of potential prey than do lakes and reservoirs.

In larger rivers, largemouth bass shift locations with the seasons. In late spring, gizzard shad, minnows, and other baitfish move through cuts to feed on plankton, invertebrates, and organic material in productive backwaters. Postspawn largemouths hold on weededges or woodcover to attack passing prey. When rivers become muddy and high, shad are pushed toward the shoreline. Shad also concentrate in thin bands that typically form along shorelines of muddy rivers and in shoreline eddies, where they feed on plankton that accumulates there. In summer, some bass move to the edges of river channels to join walleyes, catfish, smallmouths, and other river predators for a feast of shad, herring, and baby drum. Wing dams, pilings, and navigational towers in midstream hold bass on their downstream sides, but most big-river largemouths remain in backwaters year-round.

In tidal rivers, they move downstream as tides ebb, to prey on the sea life swept in on earlier tides: sandworms, eels, crabs, and saltwater baitfish like juvenile shad, herring, killifish, and silversides.

The often warm and highly fertile waters flowing from culverts and drainage pipes stimulate the growth of algae, plankton, invertebrates, milfoil, and duckweed, in turn attracting baitfish. Bass won't be far behind.

Special Effects

WEATHER CONCERNS

So far, we've concentrated on locating largemouth bass in their watery—or icy—world, disclosing their locations at different times of the year in different types of waters. Chapter 11 considers other effects on largemouths' location: wind, air pressure, and edge effects. All of them affect where you'll find and catch bass.

WIND

Temperature variations at different levels of the atmosphere produce winds. Just above and below the equator, winds typically blow from east to west—these are the trade winds that powered the sailing ships of premodern mercantile fleets. North of the 40th parallel, which runs across North

America from Redding, California, through Denver, Indianapolis, and Philadelphia, winds blow predominately west to east. These are the westerlies that come out of the Sierras and Rockies to whip across the western plains, gathering momentum as they cross the Central region and sweep over the Great Lakes to the east. Directional winds create water currents. And, although most anglers overestimate the importance of wind-induced currents, there's no question that understanding the effects of prevailing winds can be useful in locating bass.

CORIOLIS FORCE

When to westerlies is added the Coriolis force, which causes air and water to deflect clockwise in the northern hemisphere, anglers' common observation that currents move to the right of wind direction is readily explained. In immense lakes like Ontario and Superior, the current bends as much as 45 degrees. On smaller lakes, the angle of current deflection is smaller; currents tend to follow main-lake shorelines and to circle large bays in the direction of prevailing winds. Limnologists studying 9,600-acre, 80-foot-deep Lake Mendota, Wisconsin, have found that currents there are deflected about 20 degrees to the right of the wind. It's safe to assume, then, that in most lakes, the current's deflection is slightly to the right of the prevailing wind.

What are the likely effects of this discovery on locating and catching largemouth bass?

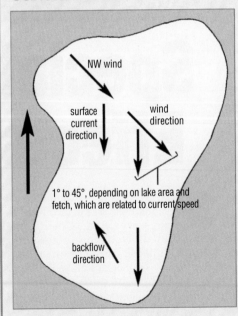

Coriolis Force

NW wind

surface
current
direction

wind
direction

1° to 45°, depending on lake area and fetch, which are related to current speed

backflow
direction

The surface of the earth spins at about 66,600 miles per hour. (Gravity keeps us from flying off the face of the earth.) This velocity affects the direction in movement for all objects. Drain a bathtub in the northern hemisphere, and the water swishes down in a clockwise direction (reversed on the other side of the equator). Winds and water currents tend to circle in the same direction.

In the northern hemisphere, wind-caused currents move to the right of wind direction. The amount of deflection is related to the size of the lake. Maximum deflection of 45° occurs only in the ocean or the world's largest lakes.

Degree of deflection increases with current speed, which is affected by wind speed only up to a critical point of 14 to 18 mph. Stronger winds don't speed currents or increase the angle of Coriolis deflection.

Currents rebound after contacting shorelines and are again deflected in a clockwise direction in the northern hemisphere. In a huge lake, the result often is one or more vast circular currents flowing clockwise.

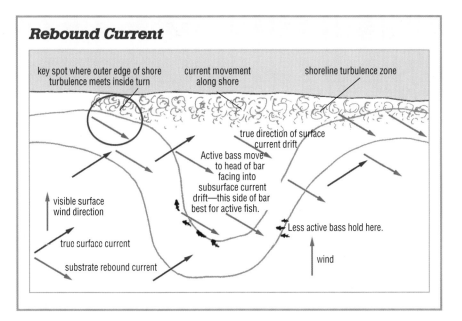

Rebound Current

key spot where outer edge of shore turbulence meets inside turn

current movement along shore

shoreline turbulence zone

true direction of surface current drift

Active bass move to head of bar facing into subsurface current drift—this side of bar best for active fish.

visible surface wind direction

true surface current

substrate rebound current

Less active bass hold here.

wind

REBOUND CURRENTS

Rebound current affects largemouths' position near middepth structural elements. Fish in shallow water usually face into shallow surface current. But fish holding deeper than about 5 feet are likely to face into a reverse current—in other words, in the opposite direction. The direction that they're facing affects your presentation. Largemouths ambush or chase their prey, so sneaking up on them from behind, without factoring in current direction, isn't likely to be successful. When bass face into the rebound current, which moves in the direction opposite to the wind, your presentation should move toward or quarter in front of them.

Main-lake structures that constrict the flow of wind-generated currents often attract baitfish and bass. A hump that rises to within a few feet of surface can compress and accelerate wind-driven currents enough to stimulate avid feeding. On smaller reservoirs, wind currents are less important. Coves on these bodies of water usually have no detectable wind currents at all, unless winds last for several days. When this happens, floating plankton may concentrate near downwind shores. Such banquets attract baitfish. Their uninvited guests are bass.

SHORELINE CURRENTS

When currents hit shorelines, they, too, are deflected clockwise. In turn, this deflection affects fishes' positions and locations. Suppose you're fishing a plateau reservoir in warm weather. Wind blowing toward the shore produces a right-moving current. If you follow the shoreline drop-off to the right until you encounter a bar, the inside turn on the current side of the bar is likely to hold active bass. If this scenario occurs in early spring or late fall, however, when water is cold and bass aren't active, the inside turn on the current side is apt to be empty. Largemouths are likely to be on the backside of the point's tip, away from the cold current. Use your knowledge of current deflection and rebound currents to locate bass.

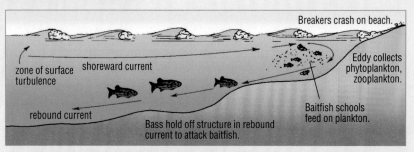

Predator Position

Breakers crash on beach.

zone of surface turbulence

shoreward current

rebound current

Bass hold off structure in rebound current to attack baitfish.

Eddy collects phytoplankton, zooplankton.

Baitfish schools feed on plankton.

Many factors affect the direction and strength of wind-caused current, so anglers must understand the physical principles, then assess conditions as they occur in a lake. Areas where current turns abruptly form eddies, where water follows a circular course. Islands, humps, and shorelines are obvious current breaks that often cause upwind eddies.

Strong directional currents collect debris and organisms incapable of strong swimming. Baitfish, including shad, yellow perch, bluegills, and shiners, may quickly congregate to feed on abundant plankton. Larger predators also appear and may hold offshore, facing into the rebound current, or may invade the turbulent shallows to chase prey.

BAROMETRIC PRESSURE

One of the most persistent traditions in fishing is that barometric pressure controls the activity level of fish. Like a lot of theories, this one is basically untestable and therefore unprovable, because whatever effects barometric changes may have on largemouths are compounded by changes in wind, temperature, and sky conditions.

When barometric pressure drops, cloud cover typically increases and weather fronts bring wind changes. When pressure rises again, blue skies, sunlight, and cooler, drier winds predominate. Largemouths definitely respond to such complexes of weather-related events—but which ones? No scientific studies have been able to demonstrate conclusively that barometric pressure alone is responsible for any changes in largemouths' behavior. One study often cited is Dr. Carl Quertermus' and George Mitchell's 1982 observation that largemouth bass in shallow water (4½ feet or less) are more likely to be found under docks when barometric pressure is high.

Atmospheric pressure usually rises after passage of a cold front, and with it return clear skies, bright sunlight, and increased ultraviolet radiation. Fish holding shallow at such times may instinctively move under docks to hide in the shade. Are they responding to barometric pressure by seeking out a new equilibrium depth, adjusting to stronger light levels, or making some other accommodation to changing conditions?

EDGE EFFECTS

Ecologists use the term "edge effect" to describe the attraction exerted on animals by places where two or more habitats come together. Such places have powerful effects on both terrestrial and aquatic creatures. These zones offer the best (and sometimes the worst) of two worlds: more cover, more prey, more potential mates, more of everything than can any single habitat.

Equipped with an underwater camera (see Chapter 12) or scuba gear, you'll recognize edges immediately. Most lakes, rivers, reservoirs, pits, or ponds may seem almost devoid of life. Upon closer inspection, however, the flat featureless areas of most lakes, ponds, rivers, reservoirs, and pits show attractive bottom change—a bed of moss; a pile of rocks; a sunken tree; a flooded stump; an isolated patch of cabbage or coontail. These may not seem like much, but to bass they represent a change in habitat and so represent opportunity. Hiding places, breeding grounds, and 24/7 sources of food.

Some edges aren't even visible to the angler who investigates under water. How can you pinpoint a spot where the light level changes from Yes to No for a bass? How to characterize the location of the thermocline, or the place where dissolved oxygen drops below the 3 parts per million necessary for a largemouth's respiration? Yet such environmental edges are everywhere. Learn to find them and you'll probably locate bass. You'll also come to admire even more the largemouth's toughness and adaptability.

WEEDEDGES

In this volume as well as its predecessor, *Largemouth Bass Fundamentals*, we talk a lot about weededges. With the expansion of vegetation in Southern and Central region reservoirs, weededges have grown in importance for bass. Like other black bass species, largemouths are opportunistic feeders that take advantage of edges to capture prey. Because of their maneuverable body shape, bass can hold motionless on the edge of a deep weedbed, fin through the transition between a shallow inside weededge and a dense, deeper outside one, or reverse to get a better look at a crayfish skittering across bottom. They lurk along edges, scouting for passing pods of bluegills or schools of shiners overhead. From their concealment, they lunge into open areas to seize prey. They also form small groups that actively search for prey along weededges. They swim and stop, peering into pockets, hoping to flush out bottom-hugging preyfish like crawfish, bullheads or yellow perch. All the bass in a group may gain a meal from this group-feeding strategy. To locate largemouths, in other words, you need to understand the uses they make of edges of every sort.

Underwater and emergent weedpatches have three edges: inside (shoreline-facing), outside (basin-facing), and overhead (canopy). Depending mostly on the season, bass will make use of one edge more than the others.

Whether they're deep or shallow, breaks in vegetation are prime bass spots.

Lake Weededge—High-Percentage Spots

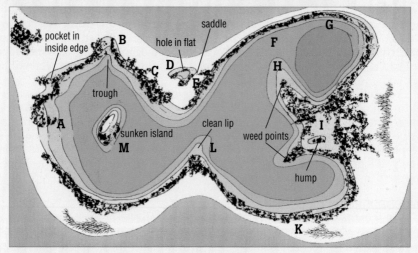

A—Widely spaced, uneven contour lines foster a jagged weededge; look for points, pockets, lots of bass-holding cover.

B—Troughs or "funnels" are prime feeding areas and migration routes for bass.

C—Check inside edges on large flats. An inside edge can hold more bass than an outside edge.

D—A 10-foot-deep hole on a flat—this is a bass magnet.

E—Hole near the drop-off creates a saddle, always attractive to fish.

F—Close, straight contour lines usually mean weed walls. Fish quickly by cranking parallel to the wall. Inside edges aren't as likely to hold fish.

G—A tight inside bend, a likely area for a curved weed wall. Search for active bass.

H—Weedy points near a deep hole must be checked for weed clumps just off the main weedlines.

I—Hump on a flat, an excellent shallow bass attractor.

J—A large flat usually offers a variety of structural elements that attract and hold bass.

K—A small flat, not likely to hold many bass, in contrast to **J**.

L—A clean lip where weeds end abruptly and the point slopes gradually toward the drop-off.

M—A big offshore hump (sunken island) offering these fine weededge possibilities: sloping point; small clean lip; sharp drop for weed wall; wider contours for a jagged weededge; possibility of thick clumps on sloping, main-lake side; and a bald spot on top.

OUTSIDE EDGES

As you drive your boat shoreward from the open main basin of a lake or reservoir, watch your sonar. Cover is often signaled by a distinct rise in bottom—a break in depth that gives rise to weedstalks, stumps, or standing timber. In natural lakes and many reservoirs and ponds, waters created by low dams, weedbeds often form green walls by midsummer, wherever bottom content isn't too hard for plants to take root. The depth of these plants' outside edge usually depends on water clarity; photosynthesis only occurs where light can penetrate water. In clear water, the outside edge may be as deep as 12 to 20 feet. In stained water, it may be only 5 to 8 feet. Such edges are likely to harbor largemouths from mid-summer into early fall, particularly if they occur on pockets, points, and bends.

INSIDE EDGES

Earlier in the season, outside edges attract few bass. That's because large-mouths, like their prey, prefer the warm shallows before the main lake heats up. They'll hold just within the inside weededge until conditions drive their prey toward shore, then follow them in. They'll build their spawning beds near inside weededges and use the edges for cover.

Inside edges aren't as obvious from a boat as outside ones. To locate them, you'll have to motor across emergent plants until they thin near shore. Often the inside edge lies in 3 or 4 feet of water, where substrate and depth change to those that can't support plants. Inside edges, particularly in the North, are dynamic. Wind action and pressure from sheet ice push sand and gravel onto shorelines, smothering emergent plants. In the Far North, a 3-foot cover of ice, when it swells and cracks, can pluck vegetation from the bottom.

In reservoirs, the location of inside weededges is sometimes determined by annual drawdowns. Flood-control impoundments are typically lowered in fall and kept low all winter in anticipation of spring floods. During these times, the drying action of sun, wind, and freezing (in northern latitudes) kills off plants on exposed shoreline beaches. Seeds or plant particles above the drawdown may remain in the sediment until springtime reflooding; if these germinate or revive, the resulting plants will constitute the new inside weededge once the reservoir refills.

Many bass anglers believe you won't find bass on inside weededges once summer arrives, but bass continue to feed on shallow flats under low-light conditions. Prey—including sunfish, young perch, and schools of shiners—are abundant in shallow, 2- to 4-foot sandy areas with sparse sandgrass or reed cover. Also abundant are bass.

They often hold on the inside edge of major weedlines on main-lake areas. On calm days, they may cruise the inside edges looking for food. Watch for them along inside edges at least 4 feet deep if the water is clear, or 2 feet if it's murky.

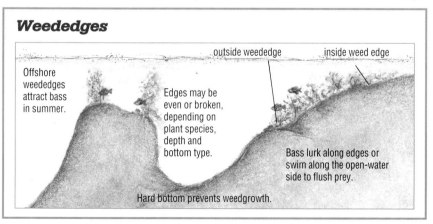

Weededges

outside weededge   inside weed edge

Offshore weededges attract bass in summer.

Edges may be even or broken, depending on plant species, depth and bottom type.

Bass lurk along edges or swim along the open-water side to flush prey.

Hard bottom prevents weedgrowth.

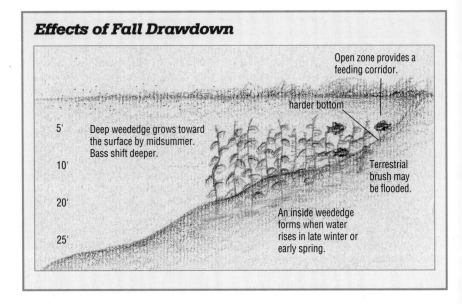

Effects of Fall Drawdown

Open zone provides a feeding corridor.

harder bottom

5' Deep weededge grows toward the surface by midsummer. Bass shift deeper.

10'

Terrestrial brush may be flooded.

20'

An inside weededge forms when water rises in late winter or early spring.

25'

EDGES WITHIN EDGES

Edges within habitat exert an attraction on animals, too. Wherever there's a change in conditions—whether of temperature, dissolved oxygen, light, bottom, structure, or vegetation—within weedgrowth, you've got another edge. We call such locations "edges within edges." Say you spot a vast, cabbage-covered flat. Within this field of cabbage appear clumps of the denser weed, coontail. Such coontail clumps often attract bass to a greater degree than expansive cabbage. If the conditions are reversed, and a small colony of cabbage grows within a field of coontail, that cabbage—that "edge within edges"—will also attract more bass. Focusing on edges-within-edges can yield incredible concentrations of bass.

OFFSHORE WEEDEDGES

It's usual to think of weededges as located near shorelines. But particularly in reservoirs that have flooded hilly terrain or large natural lakes, offshore weed-edges atop humps are common. These humps offer suitable substrate and rise to within about 10 feet of the surface—shallow enough to support a thick growth of vegetation. Bass are more likely to hold next to such humps than over them, unless the top is at least 4 feet below the surface and offers thick weedgrowth. Because such "edges" break up otherwise homogeneous stretches of water, they attract bass in summer, when their deeper offshore locations offer cooler, more oxygenated water. But the farther offshore such humps are, the longer it will take bass to find and colonize them.

OVERHEAD WEEDEDGES: SLOP BAYS

"Slop bays" develop when rooted weeds become fully grown during summer. Nutrients become available for filamentous algae, which lie in vast tangles on the surface. These clot around rooted vegetation like lily pads and wild rice, forming a floating canopy that's in effect another weededge. Beneath it, bass, from yearlings to trophies, hover amid the green murk, ambushing whatever prey happens along above them. The green jungle around them makes it difficult to chase preyfish, so "slop bass" are finely attuned to surface activity. They use their keen vision, hearing, and lateral line perception to sense moving objects above them that might become food.

In the North, bass can tolerate the warmest temperatures found in slop bays and may remain in them until fall. Slop bays in the North are often heavy with wild rice and may host the biggest largemouths of the summer; but in the South, temperatures in the slop can reach 95°F, pushing summer bass out into cooler open water. But they may return once water temperature declines.

EDGES ANGLERS MISS

SHALLOW PIVOT POINTS

In natural lakes, a primary drop-off often extends all the way around the lake, sometimes at a single depth. This depth is often but not always where rooted weedgrowth gives way to the open basin. Some lakes are deep enough to have secondary drop-offs into deeper water. They may also have underwater humps. Both have liplike upper edges that concentrate fish.

In some cases, the deep weedline and primary drop-off don't coincide. This usually occurs where light penetration is insufficient for weeds to grow to the tip of the drop-off, or where a change in bottom prevents weeds from rooting. This condition forms a double pivot point. Either or both can be a prime edge for concentrating bass.

WEEDLINES WITH JAGGED EDGES

Pockets and secondary points in weedlines are breaks in cover—another form of environmental edge. These are high-percentage areas for bass searching for prey. Less-active bass hold in the pockets, conserving energy and waiting to strike. Broken weedlines contain more bass-holding areas than solid weededges. To locate them, look for curvy contour lines on maps; jagged weedlines often follow them. Straight weed-walls mirror straight-running contour lines on lake maps. Bottom beneath jagged weedlines may be irregular and thus provide appropriate substrate for weeds in only some spots.

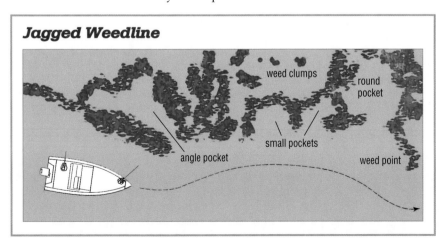

Jagged Weedline

weed clumps
round pocket
angle pocket
small pockets
weed point

Shallow Pivot Points vs. Deep Water Cradles

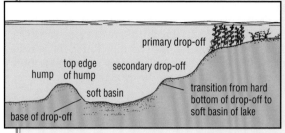

primary drop-off

top edge
hump of hump   secondary drop-off

soft basin

base of drop-off

transition from hard
bottom of drop-off to
soft basin of lake

In natural lakes, usually a primary drop-off extends all the way around the lake, often at a predominant depth level. This depth often but not always forms the boundary between rooted weedgrowth and the open basin.

Some lakes are deep enough for secondary drop-offs in deeper water. They may also have underwater humps. Both have lip-type upper edges to concentrate walleyes. Very deep structure, however, often falling below a summer thermocline, will more likely attract walleyes in fall and winter.

Note the cradle-type collection points at the base of the drop-off and where the hard bottom of the drop-off meets the basin of the lake. Subtle compared to lipped pivot areas, they nevertheless concentrate bass under the right conditions.

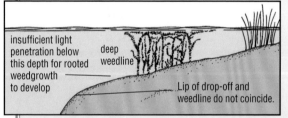

insufficient light
penetration below   deep
this depth for rooted   weedline
weedgrowth
to develop

Lip of drop-off and
weedline do not coincide.

In some cases, the deep weedline and primary drop-off don't coincide. This usually occurs where light penetration is insufficient for weeds to grow all the way out to the drop-off, or where a change in bottom type prevents weeds from rooting. This condition forms a double pivot point. Either or both can be prime concentration levels for bass.

Shallow pivot points, forming the border between the food-producing flats and the open basin of the lake, are usually lips where the depth changes distinctly. Imagine you're standing on the top edge of the Grand Canyon with your toes hanging out over nothing but a Wiley E. Coyote high dive. Get the picture? Life on the edge.

Other forms of pivot points are deep edges of cover like weeds or wood. So are top lips of humps or river channels—precipices that form a boundary between the shallows and the depths.

Many anglers fish pivot points; fewer fish deep water edges at the base of structural elements. These tend to be concave, like a cupped hand holding water; they cradle fish that drop to the bottom of the structure. The base of a drop-off, the transition to the soft bottom of a basin, or the bottom of a river channel form deep concentration edges that collect fish—usually schooled fish. If you stepped off the Grand Canyon, you'd go

Edges tend to be jagged where the bottom drops off gradually. Weeds fade away, rather than ending in the walls you encounter on steep drop-offs. To locate such edges, you'll need polarized sunglasses. Many plant species will not grow much deeper than 10 feet. Hydrilla, however, may extend to the surface in more than 20 feet of water. Know your plant species and seek out their irregular weed-edges: These concentrate bass.

on a wild slide before bottoming out at the base of the drop-off. If there wasn't a distinct cradle at bottom—more of a curve, like a playground slide— you'd always roll out across bottom before coming to rest, just like a bass moving out to the transition between hard and soft bottom.

Concentration areas aren't always depth changes or cover. The deepest penetration of sunlight forms an edge that fish can relate to. So does the top of a summer thermocline, an artificial bottom that fish remain above. Not a lip, but a cradle that fish encounter as they drop into the depths. Fish that suspend may move to open water at these levels, too.

Pivot points—edges where fish make the transition from schooling to scattering—can be the sites of aggressive feeding. Deep cradles are more conducive to schooled fish, which are

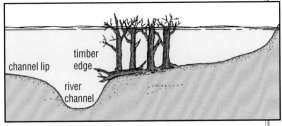

level of light penetration

thermocline

intersections with slope

Sloping shorelines with no distinct depth changes or cover may lack obvious pivot points. In this case, factors like light penetration or the presence of a thermocline determine how deep bass will be if they use the area. Fish may favor other spots with more distinct structure.

timber edge

channel lip

river channel

In shallow impoundments, distinct river channels often cut across shallow flats. The top lip of the channel usually is a focal point of fish activity, with or without timber, depending on conditions. Fish that move shallower tend to scatter across the flat or into the timber. Note also that bass in deep water could lie at the base of the channel, cradled along the edge.

often less aggressive. While we focus here on pivot points, locating and fishing deep cradles is similar. Pivot points tend to be areas of major activity during the warmwater season. Cradles tend to be better during coldwater periods of the year, but they're always worth checking if pivot points don't produce.

PHANTOM WEEDEDGES

Be on the lookout for tufts of weeds outside weedwall edges. These are not readily visible because they grow only 4 to 5 feet off bottom. Anglers often hold off points, casting to weededges, unaware that they're floating above the best spots of all. By the time they look at their depthfinders and see the telltale broken red lines or gray clouds on the LCD, the fish have already spooked and scattered.

On lakes where such phantom weededges are common, bottom is often stair-stepped outside the visible weededge. Pockets on phantom weededges allow bass to move inward to feed and then retire to back areas, always remaining close to cover.

WEEDLESS EDGES

Suddenly an opening looms in the weededge. It's emphatic, not just a small break in a continuous edge. This is another variation on the "edge within edges." Those may be natural breaks, or caused by dredging or weed removal.

Isolated breaks often hold more bass than weededges that are fuller and more lush. As unpromising as such barren spots might seem, it's the change an edge represents that constitutes its attraction for fish, not what lies on either side of it. Bass in particular are edge-oriented—it's where they feed most efficiently. So, energize yourself by fishing the edge effect.

Other Environmental Edges Anglers Often Miss

The Surface—The Water-Air Interface—Possibly this is the most obvious and overlooked edge of all. Everything that falls into and climbs out of the water passes through and often pauses on the surface. This is the edge where oxygen levels are greatest, where water temperatures most quickly rise and fall, where noises can attract or repel, and where the surface can be ruffled by wind to diffuse light, or calmed down to allow it to penetrate deeper into the water column. In this air-water interface, especially in early summer, muskies, bass, and lake trout often are found basking in the tepid water just under the surface. It's where ice forms in winter and where two different worlds collide.

The Land-Water-Air Interface—Everything mentioned above applies equally here, only throw in a third world colliding: The terrestrial environment. Ever wonder why we motor halfway down a lake, river, or reservoir, pull up close to an island or the main-lake shoreline, and cast a topwater lure as close to the bank as we possibly can throw it?

Moon Phases—There is a reason why a disproportionate number of world-record fish have been caught during shortlived monthly moon phases. It's the same reason muskie anglers time their seasonal trips and the reason bass come in to spawn. Lunar periods affect fish activity levels. Indeed, they control ocean tides, perhaps the greatest factor influencing saltwater fish behavior. All moon periods can be hot, but the monthly full moon and dark moon phases usually are the most eagerly anticipated by anglers.

Cold Current Edges—Cold currents may arise from deep-water upwellings, when lake water is pushed through a narrows or some other constriction, or where a cooler stream flows into a warm lake or reservoir. In summer, cold current edges can refresh. In early spring, late fall, and winter, though, especially for warmwater fish, upwellings can be an edge they avoid.

Other Edges . . . (cont.)

Warmwater Discharges—A warm, fertile river spilling into a cold, infertile trout lake, or a shallow, balmy creek trickling into a cold, deep river are warmwater currents that attract fish. The rich, tepid water encourages the growth of lush plants and algae, attracts schools of baitfish, and creates a resort-like environment for sportfish. These warm, hospitable environmental edges can be at their best for trout, bass, walleyes, muskies, pike, and panfish during the coldwater periods of early spring, late fall, and winter. Manmade warmwater edges—usually discharges from electrical generating facilities—produce the same desirable effects.

Underwater Springs—Trout require cool water with plenty of oxygen in order to survive. In spring, fall, and winter, trout spread throughout a river or reservoir. But the dog days of summer create considerable stress. They also create perfect conditions for locating schools of bunched up trout that in turn attract big bass. The key is finding environmental edges that create ideal living conditions, like a tiny brush-covered, spring-fed creek that trickles into a larger river. Or a boiling artesian spring that bubbles up from the stream bed and draws trout to its edges. Find that same hidden spring or upwelling in a lake or reservoir, and you'll find fish throughout the warm-weather months.

Night Lights—Lights on piers and docks may be manmade, but the insects and bugs they attract are natural. Watch out for diminishing returns, though. One lone, isolated light on a dock can be ten times better than ten lights on ten docks.

Chapter 12

Electronic Aids

Tools for Fine-tuning Bass Location

UNDERWATER UNDERSTANDING

In this chapter, we examine recent developments in sense-expanding technologies—many of them first developed for the military—that can extend your awareness of bass behavior and location.

FISH-WATCHING

The human eye and brain are as sensitive, in their way, as the bass's are in theirs. If you want to learn more about largemouths' location, start with the two fish finders on the front of your head. Bass make this relatively easy, since they spend much of the early part of the season in shallow water and often remain visible at other times, at least in clear habitats. To help you get started doing some serious fish watching, meet Ralph Manns of Austin, Texas, a fishery scientist and angling authority who has written for *In-Fisherman* magazine for over two decades.

Manns became a dedicated bass watcher while studying fish biology and fishery management at Southwest Texas State University. He often sat atop a high bank overlooking one of the many ponds at the university's Aquatic Science Facility. With polarized sunglasses, Manns learned to spot inactive bass lying motionless near bottom. Doing so presented something of a challenge, since some of the ponds were clear, others murky, still others full of cover. But his vigilance and patience paid off—he learned things about bass behavior that hadn't been mentioned in his classroom studies. He found that the official line that "bass ambush prey from inside cover," for example, should be heavily qualified.

What Manns observed can be important to your locating and catching bass: "The reality is that most active, catchable bass are cruising along cover edges or moving under lines of cover in a series of starts and stops. Once this behavior is seen and understood, it's possible to make better decisions on where to cast or how soon to return to a productive spot," he says.

"Bass that are hidden in cover and apparently inactive usually ignore minnows tossed nearby. After several minnows swim within easy striking range, bass seem to awaken and start feeding. The appearance of many prey nearby gives bass a cue to leave cover and hunt."

Manns' early observations were verified when he donned scuba gear in Travis Reservoir to watch bass. "While diving, we saw totally inactive bass inside cover, apparently digesting food and ignoring nearby preyfish hovering within inches of their snouts. Semi-active bass that were suspended near cover or drifting about would attack only prey that were both nearby and vulnerable, ignoring healthy sunfish just a few feet away.

"Bass hunt actively, usually moving in small schools along the shoreline and edges of cover. They enter cover to rest, hide from larger predators, and digest food. They sometimes strike nearby prey targets that are lulled into approaching too close or that get careless. These behaviors may account for great catches made by carefully flipping or pitching lures into cover."

Manns' decades of bass watching taught him how to elicit strikes from these fish: "When a lure looks and moves like a healthy preyfish, it must be close to a bass to be considered a vulnerable target. Bass learn early in life that healthy, alert prey can successfully dodge them. They learn to conserve energy and await vulnerable targets. To consistently draw strikes, a lure must appear to be fleeing in panic, to be trapped against a solid background, injured or distracted, and unaware of the bass.

"For too long, writers and biologists have emphasized the ambushing nature of bass. Take time to look and study for yourself," Manns advises. "You'll see what bass observers have seen. And you'll likely reach similar conclusions." To test Manns' thesis and to make your own, you'll need to regularly visit sites where bass can be observed.

In today's scientific world, field research has declined somewhat in recent decades, replaced by laboratory research and computer modeling that emphasize quantifiable data that can be tested statistically. Not surprisingly, the latter doesn't focus much on fish behavior. Even telemetry studies tend to focus on home-range sizes and movement distances. If you're more interested in daily activity patterns or how fish search and locate prey, it may be time to get out on the water and watch these behaviors for yourself. What you witness and learn may be remarkable, as the following account demonstrates.

Several years ago, Manns found himself engaged in a new field project when he found a skinny, 20-inch female largemouth hanging along the shoreline of a large pond behind his home. Struck by her poor condition, Manns began tossing her fish fillets, dead shad, and meat cut in the shape of a Slug-Go.

"Within a week, she learned to see food in the air and to intercept it when it hit the water. Feeding noises quickly attracted other bass and created competition. Within days, I was feeding five or six bass daily, watching them compete for each morsel. The creation of a special spot where food was routinely abundant and available made territoriality easy to see.

"The biggest bass ruled. She tended to hold facing the shore in the prime spot where most of the tossed shad landed. Other bass were forced away if they ventured closer than about 4 feet.

Territorial Spacing

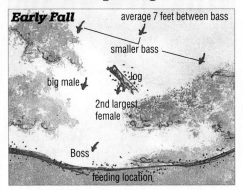

Bass were fairly active and moved periodically. The big male was aggressive, chasing away smaller bass including the second-largest female.

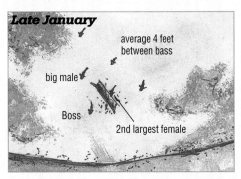

Bass almost immobile. They only moved a few feet to feed and did not cruise.

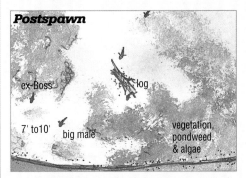

The big male came back from spawning in an aggressive mood, dominating the old "boss" bass for several weeks. The soon-to-be-dominant female had yet to return.

At times, when I wasn't tossing shad, she left her key spot and cruised around a 20-foot-wide circle, but she guarded the prime location.

"Boss didn't have to actually attack the lower-ranked bass. Simply turning toward them usually was enough to run them off. During the brief moments when they competed for a shad, however, the rules of territory were forgotten. They reappeared as soon as a food item was gone. Smaller and faster bass often dashed ahead of the larger bass to steal food but raced back to their positions 4 to 8 feet to the rear and to either side of larger bass. After one or two such thefts, the big fish often became more aggressive and chased the smaller bass farther away. But leaving her key spot to chase others often resulted in the dominant bass getting fewer shad, if I tossed food at regular intervals.

"Biological theory has postulated that larger fish swim faster and are stronger than smaller fish of the same species. This may be true of species that retain their streamlined shape as they grow. But larger bass become slower as they gain in bulk and become less streamlined, even though they have more muscle. This forces lunker females, as they grow, to isolate from smaller fish, school less, and become more territorial."

Manns' observations were made using nothing more complicated than polarized sunglasses. Stan Gerzsenyi, a professional bass angler, scuba dives to observe bass behavior. When not competing or guiding, he often slips into the water to watch bass behavior, position, and relationship to cover.

Ralph Manns

Bass Pro Stan Gerzenyi monitors bass behavior by scuba diving and with an underwater camera.

Like Manns, Gerzsenyi has challenged an article of faith among bass anglers with his patient observations. Based on what he's witnessed on dives and on the underwater videos he's made, he's convinced that pros' belief that "if they can just find the bass, they can catch them," amounts to little more than wishful thinking. Gerzsenyi's dives revealed bass on practically every point or piece of cover that a typical bass angler would normally fish. The problem wasn't lack of bass—they were spread throughout productive bassing waters—but the fishes' unwillingness to strike.

On average, Gerzsenyi reports, it took many casts near several bass to elicit a hit. He suggests that hits come from only some 10 percent of the bass that anglers cast to. Typically, many neutral fish are present on each piece of good structure, and they won't bite unless a lure travels close to them and maybe not even then. Some inactive or neutral bass can be stimulated by repeat casts nearby. The real challenge for bass fisherman, Gerzsenyi concludes, is not finding bass—it's finding fish active enough to strike.

The Aqua-Vu DVR (Digital Video Recorder) allows viewers to record and store underwater discoveries and replay them for entertainment and learning purposes.

UNDERWATER CAMERAS

In-Fisherman founder Al Lindner has been a fan of underwater cameras since testing them in the late 1990s. "After scouting with an Aqua-Vu, my mind is alive with new places to take it," he states. "I thought I had a pretty good idea of what structures looked like. So, I was shocked to see how wrong I'd been about some spots."

Minnesota fishing pro Ted Capra echoes Lindner's enthusiasm. "Underwater cameras are one of the most important new tools for anglers since sonar. I've wondered why I've caught fish on only one side of a bar, and now I know. Does the camera give anglers an unfair advantage? Typically, if I view a spot and see 10 or 20 fish, I may catch a few of them. But at times, schools seem uncatchable.There's no way to make fish bite. When I first started scouting I caught lots fewer fish, because I spent more time looking and less time fishing."

Today, underwater viewing systems are available with features like lights for night viewing and enhanced camera positioning systems. Many are available for less than the cost of a good sonar or trolling motor, or about the same as a top-of-the line reel.

We've found that cameras don't spook bass as was initially reported. Rather, they often seem curious, swimming up to investigate the apparatus. Closely examining specific cover objects on favorite spots demonstrates that subtle characteristics attract big bass, while other nearly identical areas remain lifeless. We've discovered that it isn't odd to spot bass roaming well above the bottom, sometimes far from cover objects. We also learned that bass do indeed swim down to chase prey.

Beyond mysteries solved, underwater viewing during fishing trips brings an immediate boost of confidence, whether you're exploring a new lake or preparing for tournament competition. Accurate visualization spawns this confidence, a mindset that inevitably yields more fish.

SONAR

In 1957, Carl Lowrance began marketing his original Red Box and Green Box. Using a technology developed for the military, sonar has since taught generations of anglers how to locate fish and how to interpret bottom features represented by various models.

Does sonar technology help anglers locate more fish? That depends on how well it's understood and used. Without factoring in all the other elements covered in this book, a sonar display won't get you very far—you'll be too busy checking out unproductive parts of the lake and then puzzling over display results, to do much productive fishing. But used as an adjunct to what your eyes tell you about lake or river structure, weather, water temperature, and where fish are in relation to the Calendar Period, sonar units can fine-tune the task of locating largemouths.

Original sonars used a lighted wheel, called a flasher. Paper graphs soon followed, drawing intricate pictures of the bottom and fish. Many anglers found them difficult to operate and maintain, however. Yet avid structure fishermen recognized them as far more accurate than other methods.

The market for sonar is driven not by the few professionals but by the large market of amateurs. As a result, sonar manufacturers have abandoned paper graphs entirely, and only a few of them continue to build flashers. Even after two decades of refining liquid crystal displays (LCDs), manufacturers know that flashers penetrate matted vegetation better than LCDs. They're also easier to tune, and most of them provide reliable depth-readings at speeds of more than 60 mph.

LCD units have now come a long way, with greatly improved picture definition, thanks to new screen technologies. New electronic circuitry has improved the speed of readings, approaching "real time." The latest generation includes new colored displays featuring TFT technologies (thin film transistors) that enhance screen clarity in bright sunlight. Each pixel has its own transistor, allowing the unit to provide a full scale of 256 color variations. This technology is the same as in your flat-screen TV. Here's what to look for in LCD units, and how to tune and interpret them to get the most relevant information.

Lowrances' original "Green Box" is a collector's item but some remain in use today.

TRANSDUCERS

For most anglers, transducers are those things mounted on the back of boats or placed somewhere in their hulls. They get blamed for poor images, poor high-speed performance, and no picture. But if you know how these small but important objects work and how to make them work better, they will become the objects of interest they deserve to be.

All transducers have one thing in common: They contain a crystal that vibrates in response to electrical current. The crystal converts that current to sound energy, which is emitted at a particular frequency and direction. In the case of fishing sonar, the operating frequency from 50 kHz to 400 kHz is aimed at the lake bottom. When the sound energy bounces back—whether from fish, or from bottom and other structure—it's reconverted (transduced) to electrical energy. This travels to the locator head, where it's displayed as an image. Screen images are displayed as cross-sections of depth, and objects that have impeded the sonar unit's sound waves are displayed at their respective depths.

Discussions of transducers usually center on their frequency and cone angle (beam width). Most freshwater sonar units operate in the 50- to 200-kHz range. Every frequency within this spectrum offers advantages and disadvantages. Manufacturers choose frequencies to optimize particular performances and functions. It's important to know what these are before choosing a unit.

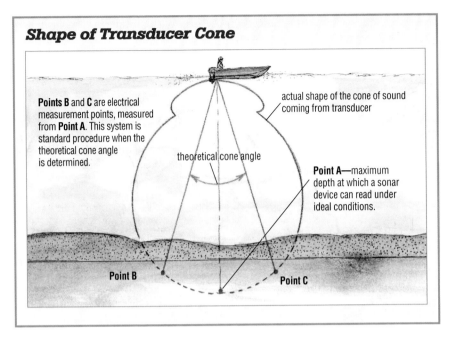

Shape of Transducer Cone

Points B and **C** are electrical measurement points, measured from **Point A**. This system is standard procedure when the theoretical cone angle is determined.

actual shape of the cone of sound coming from transducer

theoretical cone angle

Point A—maximum depth at which a sonar device can read under ideal conditions.

Point B

Point C

Cone angle or beam width refers to the diameter of the three-dimensional cone of water covered by the unit's sonar at a particular depth, which is usually referred to as the "half-power point," or –3 dB. Think of the cone angle as an inverted sugar cone, with the point as the transducer. A narrow cone angle looks like a narrow ice cream cone, while a wide cone angle looks like a broad one. Depending on frequency, cone angles typically range from about 8 to 50 degrees. Usually the cone angle is narrower at high operating frequency and broader at low frequency. These are physical limits that design can't overcome.

A narrow cone angle—say, one of fewer than 20 degrees—provides more accurate bottom detail with less coverage, while a wide cone angle displays a larger area with perhaps more targets. But those targets are spread out over a larger area, and it's unclear exactly how close they are to your boat. When you've located a fish with a narrow-beam transducer, you know that it's near or under your boat. Measured at –3 dB, an 8-degree transducer covers an area whose diameter is about 1/6 of water depth (scans a 3-foot circle in 18 feet of water); a 20-degree transducer covers an area whose diameter is about 1/3 of water depth (6-foot circle); a 38-degree transducer, one whose diameter is about 2/3 of water depth (12-foot circle).

The disadvantages of low-frequency systems are that they usually don't work well in water less than 10 to 15 feet, and that they penetrate deeper water more weakly than high-frequency systems. But a narrow-beam transducer (say, 8 degrees) can concentrate sound energy and reach deep water. In several hundred feet of water, even narrow beams penetrate to significant depths. For example, deep-water anglers on the Great Lakes often prefer low-frequency units. High-frequency systems, however, usually offer better target separation.

Because there are advantages to both designs, a few manufacturers produce sonar units able to operate at dual frequencies. A common dual frequency transducer operates at 50/200 kHz. A second design offers a dual-beam transducer whose frequency stays the same but whose cone width can be set for either 9 or 18 degrees. Yet another design is built around transducers containing multiple crystals of the same frequency; each scans in a different direction—right, left, or center—thus creating a wider beam of coverage.

TRANSDUCER POWER

Power determines how deeply sonar penetrates; a more powerful unit can send its signal deeper into water. For deep fishing, a 3,000-watt unit performs better than a 200-watt one. The latest units boast up to 8,000 watts peak-to-peak. But how much power do you need? Bottom hardness, fresh or salt water, plankton concentration, interference, and receiver sensitivity are factors affecting the depth to which a unit can penetrate.

Two aspects of sonar power should be factored into your decisions about how much sonar to buy: edge detection and target separation.

Edge detection—The strongest signal is along the axis of the transducer. On the edges of that sound cone, energy decreases. Powerful locators— sonar units— help detect targets at the edges of the cone better than less powerful ones.

Target separation—Another aspect of sonar power is a unit's ability to detect and display objects like fish, rocks, and weeds. Greater power can drive sound waves to lake bottom in deeper water, making possible the separation of objects that are close together. Most units with midrange frequency can separate targets that are about

Hard Bottom

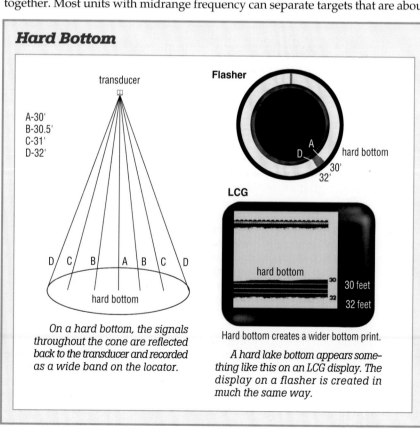

A-30'
B-30.5'
C-31'
D-32'

transducer

D C B A B C D

hard bottom

On a hard bottom, the signals throughout the cone are reflected back to the transducer and recorded as a wide band on the locator.

Flasher

A
D
hard bottom
30'
32'

LCG

hard bottom

30 feet
32 feet

Hard bottom creates a wider bottom print.

A hard lake bottom appears something like this on an LCG display. The display on a flasher is created in much the same way.

Soft Bottom

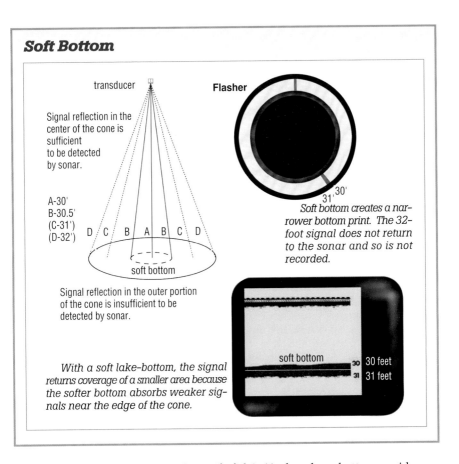

transducer

Signal reflection in the center of the cone is sufficient to be detected by sonar.

A-30'
B-30.5'
(C-31')
(D-32')

D C B A B C D

soft bottom

Signal reflection in the outer portion of the cone is insufficient to be detected by sonar.

With a soft lake-bottom, the signal returns coverage of a smaller area because the softer bottom absorbs weaker signals near the edge of the cone.

Flasher

31' 30'

Soft bottom creates a narrower bottom print. The 32-foot signal does not return to the sonar and so is not recorded.

soft bottom

30 — 30 feet
31 — 31 feet

---

3 inches apart in shallow water. That is, if a fish is 4 inches above bottom, a midrange unit can show the fish and bottom as distinct objects. But if a fish lies 2 inches off bottom, fish and bottom are likely to blend into a single image. Similarly, if your boat is floating over three fish all the same distance from the transducer, even though they're at different depths only one fish will be displayed. Target separation widens in deeper water, so the more powerful a unit is, the greater likelihood that it can bounce off bottom and separate objects in close proximity to each other.

How much edge and target separation to buy depends on where you do most of your fishing. If you rarely fish deeper than 30 feet and bottom there is relatively firm, 300 watts may be adequate for you. If you fish soft-bottomed lakes or deeper water, you'll get more satisfaction from a 2,000- to 3,000-watt unit.

PIXELS

Another important feature of LCD units is the number of pixels, or "picture elements"—those tiny squares that produce the image on your graph's screen. The vertical pixel count (VPC) determines your screen's resolution, and the better the resolution, the more detailed the display. Vertical pixels break the column of water below you into segments. The more segments, and the smaller segments it gets broken into, the more information is provided. Current VPC on most units is 200 to 500. In 30 feet of water, one pixel on a screen with a VPC

Sonar Tips

- To reduce electrical interference, wire your sonar to the starting battery or a separate battery, not to the trolling motor battery.
- Install an inline fuse.
- Ensure that nuts are tight on the connecting posts of the battery; loose connections cause countless electronic and engine problems.
- Use swivel mounting brackets, particularly on an LCG or GPS. Their screens are light-sensitive and have a narrower viewing angle compared to other electronic displays.

Turning and tilting the unit to improve screen visibility often is necessary.

- Don't travel long distances with electronics mounted; the pounding from the road does no good. Swivel mounting brackets allow for easy removal and act as shock absorbers on the road or water, cushioning the unit.
- If your boat sits in water all season, use a scouring pad (not too abrasive) to periodically clean algae from the face (bottom) of the transducer.

of 100 represents about 3.5 inches. One pixel on a screen with a VPC of 350 at the same depth represents about 1.5 inches. Horizontal pixel counts also can be important, as the screen width, along with chart speed, determines how much of the history of the underwater world remains on the screen before scrolling away. Buy as high a pixel count as you can afford. Powerful units cost more, but they're worth the price.

INTERPRETING SONAR

The problem with both deep water and soft bottom is the weak signal they return. In deep water, the signal travels a long way on its round-trip from surface to lake bottom and back to the surface again. As it travels, it becomes weaker and therefore harder to detect, translate, and display. On soft bottoms like muck and silt, much of the signal is absorbed by the substrate. To improve readings over such substrates, turn up the unit's sensitivity in manual mode to a level higher than the default one the unit's auto mode selected. In water shallower than 5 feet, the return signal can be too strong because of the short distance it travels: In this case, auto mode may not reduce the sensitivity setting enough to produce a clear picture. Instead, the whole screen may "gray out." To adjust, turn down the sensitivity in shallow water or over a hard bottom, thereby providing a narrower cone angle. In deeper water or over softer bottom, increase sensitivity to provide a broader cone angle.

Weeds provide another set of challenges for controlling sensitivity. Bass fishing along the edges of weedlines or over weedbeds is common. Locators that are set in auto mode have difficulty handling such locations. If you increase the sensitivity to penetrate to the bottom in a weedbed, the screen will be saturated and lacking in detail. Remember that increasing sensitivity raises the unit's listening ability, not the locator's power. When you power up in auto mode in dense vegetation, you get a strong return signal because vegetation is a good reflector, sending back a strong signal that lacks detail because of its multiple surfaces. Your unit is on overload. To reduce the unit's sensitivity around weeds, use the sonar in manual mode, changing its sensitivity settings several times to learn which works best.

The sensitivity control is the locator's most important function. Learn how it affects what you see on screen, so that the unit is working for and not against you. Head out to your favorite body of water and position your boat in shallow water, deep water, over hard bottom, soft bottom, over rockpiles and in front of weedlines. See how the unit reports back on each of these areas. Adjust its sensitivity settings to see how doing so affects the information displayed. Decide which work best in situations you're familiar with. Doing so will give you more confidence in your sonar's capabilities.

GLOBAL POSITIONING SATELLITE (GPS) SYSTEMS

The Global Positioning Satellite system is the most important locating technology to be introduced to fishing since the introduction of the depthfinder. GPS was developed for the U.S. Department of Defense, and its first widespread use was during the Gulf War. Drawing on a network of satellites orbiting some 11,000 miles above the earth, a GPS unit can triangulate locations for latitude and longitude to within 20 to 70 feet.

Not surprisingly, the number of anglers who own GPS units has skyrocketed. Prices have fallen and new technologies have appeared for both boat-mounted and handheld units.

Anglers use GPS for better positioning accuracy, marking spots, mapping, and charting routes within water bodies. GPS mapping systems offer electronic displays of lakes, rivers, and their shorelines. Back in the mid-90s when GPS units first appeared on the sporting goods scene, maps were cartridge-based and quite basic. They displayed freeway systems, state roads, large and mid-sized lakes, rivers, and medium to large towns. Background maps typically covered the entire U.S. as well as parts of Canada and Mexico. Greater topographic detail became available when manufacturers introduced cartridges that enhanced designated areas on background maps. These provided additional useful navigational information— buoy markers, reefs, channels, and water depths. Extent and detail of coverage varies and certain computer applications are required, so check features before you buy electronic maps.

Cartridge mapping systems are available in chart-by-chart or seamless options. The chart-by-chart method is a digital version of the paper maps you've worked with for years, and it carries with it the same problem—differences of scale when you move from one map to another. The seamless method scrolls across a map with a uniform scale.

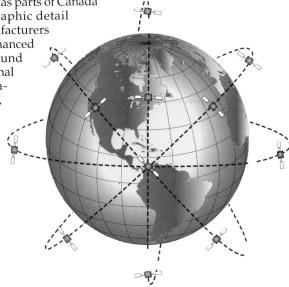

Global Positioning Satellite systems use a constellation of 24 satellites covering the earth in precise orbits about 11,000 miles out in space. As many as 12 satellites are available for signal transmission and receiver reception at any one time.

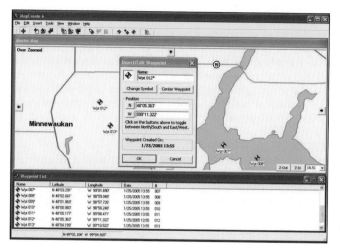

The latest GPS units allow you to manage waypoints and trails for more efficient navigation.

The quality of mapping details is a function of two factors, the electronic file in the map cartridge and the acuity of your display monitor. In the case of a typical LCD screen, the total pixel count and the screen's ability to react to light are the factors determining detail. Coarse screens may not adequately display all of the information available on a cartridge, particularly small details.

Keep in mind that zooming down to a small scale may not increase detail. It may mean instead that what you saw at 2 miles is only bigger at 0.2 mile, not more detailed. Different levels of detail should appear at different zoom or scale levels. For example, contour lines, small reefs, and islands that may not appear on a 20-mile scale should become visible on a 3-mile scale. Check to make sure that the mapping system you buy offers that capability.

The appearance of CD-ROMs in the GPS lineup means that instead of buying a handful of cartridges to cover all the areas you travel for outdoor activities, you can now cover the entire country in great detail with one or two CDs. When you load a mapping CD—such as Lowrance's MapCreate or Garmin's Road and Recreation and MetroGuide U.S.—the program appears on the monitor. Select or outline the area you want transferred to your GPS unit. The transfer is done through a data cable that attaches to the computer's data port. Mapping programs allow you to create or customize your own maps, so you can choose the details you want displayed—small streams, rural roads, restaurants, street names, navigational aids, state parks, and so on.

Once you've selected a map area for downloading, the information is transferred into a "flash memory" (typically, 2 to 8 MB of memory on a blank cartridge or MMC card that fits in your GPS unit). Depending on the level of detail you've chosen, a single file can include a state the size of Georgia.

GPS APPLICATIONS

Marking waypoints is another strength of GPS systems. You can mark important points like home port, boat ramps, rocks, and reefs on your GPS maps so that you can avoid hazards or accurately return to fishing spots again, even in bad weather or at night. Thanks to contour maps offered by such companies as Lakemaster, C-Map, Fishing Hot Spots, Lowrance, and Navionics in cartridge, CD, and website formats, you can add waypoints to existing contour maps.

When you're working on your computer with mapping systems, such as those produced by Fishing Hot Spots and Waypoint Technologies, you can move your mouse to locations and set them as waypoints. The system numbers your waypoints and you can name them for better identification. Marking underwater points, inside turns, and sunken islands is simple. This information can then be downloaded to your GPS unit.

Most GPS units let you place markers or icons on the screen to mark fish or interesting structure for future reference. Most anglers don't bother to punch in names for locations of caught fish, as they expect them to change. You can enter them on your computer later or log them into a notebook in case of GPS unit failure. GPS also is a safety feature, provided your batteries don't go dead. Even on familiar waters, anglers can become disoriented in fog, heavy rain, or other severe weather. Waypoints, icons, or saved trails can lead you to your destination. GPS has turned many shoreline casters into open-water anglers, thanks to the technology's ability to get them back home over featureless, expansive waters.

Now you're equipped with all the tools that recent technology has to offer, and you know where the fish are. Where to find the giants among them is covered in our final chapter.

Soc Clay

Lunker Bass and Where to Find Them

TROPHY FISH FINDER

Largemouths have proven to be North America's most adaptable gamefish. They've been stocked from the Atlantic to the Pacific, from Mexico to Manitoba. So, offering anglers advice on where to find the biggest largemouths is a challenge, particularly since hotspots may come and go with environmental and biological changes.

Our first advice: Fish your local ponds. The all-time biggest producers of trophy bass in In-Fisherman's Master Angler Program have not been the big "factory" reservoirs of southern California, Texas, Florida, or Mexico, but countless small farm ponds spread across North America. These small waters have yielded nearly 150 award fish. Unnamed, distinctly un-famous locations out-produce the celebrated fisheries detailed below. For example, the biggest largemouths in the Northeast—almost Texas-sized—reside in small coastal ponds in Massachusetts, while Georgia and Alabama's biggest bass (13 to 15 pounds) continue to come from private ponds. In Chapter 9, we detailed the remarkable fertility of ponds.

The biggest producers of trophy bass have been farm ponds across North America.

That said, what follows is a run-down of those reservoirs, natural lakes, and river chains that have produced dependable populations of big largemouths. The places we list below are either already-celebrated waters or ones that deserve, at a minimum, regional reputations.

The world of lunker bass has changed remarkably since the early 1970s, when southern Californians started pulling 20-pound, Florida-strain largemouths from Lake Miramar and other Golden State reservoirs. California's lunkers were first introduced in San Diego County in 1959, when the Department of Fish and Game planted 20,400 fingerling bass from Holt State Fish Hatchery, which is near Pensacola, Florida. Since then, California waters have regularly produced lunkers of a size that used to be considered exceptional. Today, Florida bass have been planted in scores of California's public waters, where they can grow huge in the temperate climate. The biggest of them reach world-record proportions.

With the exception of those other warmwater states, Florida and Texas, the rest of North America is unlikely ever to produce bass that reach the size of California's. Florida-strain bass have the potential to grow larger than their northern cousins in mild climates, and the warm, fertile habitats of California, Texas, and Florida offer them all the forage they need to grow huge. Seductive as the image of even 12- or 15-pounders in your Central or Northeastern lakes or reservoirs may be, it's unrealistic. However, as more about bass biology and management is understood, the size of bass continent-wide is increasing. Waters once too polluted to produce big bass have been cleaned up. Recently built reservoirs have had their timber left intact, providing excellent cover. In some cases, reservoir water levels have been adjusted to favor production of healthy fisheries. Stocking of catchable-sized rainbow trout into two-tier fisheries has added a high-protein food source for the largest bass. All these have encouraged fast growth for largemouth bass. In big river systems and the Great Lakes, the arrival of zebra mussels, an otherwise unfortunate event, has benefited predators like bass, muskies, and walleyes as waters have become clearer and weedier.

As a result, the world of trophy bass fishing has changed dramatically. Its center of gravity has moved away from George Perry's Georgia waters to reservoirs far to the west. Texas, Florida, and California are now the likeliest locations, followed by Louisiana, Mississippi, and Arizona. For destination anglers, California and nearby states in Mexico offer the biggest, most productive largemouth fishing of all. But notice that we say "destination anglers"—those lucky fishermen who seek out distant locations for connecting with 8- to 14-pounders. In this chapter, we'll point you toward locations that have proven themselves throughout the 1990s and into the first decade of the 21st century.

NORTH AMERICA'S TROPHY BASS PRODUCERS

In-Fisherman's Master Angler Program has offered awards for trophy-sized bass to anglers throughout North America for three decades. Awards are based on size requirements that vary across five regions, from 6.5 pounds or 22 inches in northern waters, to 10 pounds or 24 inches in the South, California, and Mexico. The nearly 2,000 trophy-sized largemouths recorded in this program reveal fascinating trends in the location and timing of big-bass bites. Program results have yielded a different lineup of powerhouse bass fisheries than, say, the Bassmaster Top 25, which is compiled on the basis of reports from the International Game Fish Association, the National Fresh Water Fishing Hall of Fame, state fishery agencies, and *Western Outdoor News*.

Top 31 Largemouths

1.	22 lbs, 4 oz (22.25 lbs)	Montgomery Lake, Georgia	George Perry	June 2, 1932
2.	22 lbs, 1/2 oz (22.01 lbs)	Lake Castaic, California	Bob Crupi	March 12, 1991
3.	21 lbs, 12 oz (21.75 lbs)	Lake Castaic, California	Mike Arujo	March 5, 1991
4.	21 lbs, 11 oz (21.7 lbs)	Lake Dixon, California	Jed Dickerson	May 31, 2003
5.	21 lbs, 3½ oz (21.19 lbs)	Lake Casitas, California	Raymond Easley	March 4, 1980
6.	21 lbs, 1/2 ounce (21.01 lbs)	Lake Castaic, California	Bob Crupi	March 9, 1990
7.	20 lbs, 15 oz (20.94 lbs)	Lake Miramar, California	David Zimmerlee	June 23, 1973
7.	20 lbs, 15 oz (20.94 lbs)	Lake Miramar, California	John Gardunu	May 25, 1990
9.	20 lbs, 14 oz (20.86 lbs)	Lake Castaic, California	Leo Torres	February 4, 1990
10.	20 lbs, 12 oz (20.75 lbs)	Lake Dixon, California	Mike Long	April 27, 2001
11.	20 lbs, 4 oz (20.25 lbs)	Lake Hodges, California	Gene Dupras	May 30, 1985
12.	20 lbs, 2 oz (20.13 lbs)	Big Fish Lake, Florida	Fritz Friebel	May, 1923
13.	19 lbs, 10 oz (19.63 lbs)	Lake Baccarac, Mexico	Bruce Newsome	January 17, 1993
14.	19 lbs, 8 oz (19.50 lbs)	Lake Miramar, California	Keith Gunsauls	March 7, 1988
15.	19 lbs, 7 oz (19.4 lbs)	Lake Dixon, California	Mac Weakley	June, 2003
16.	19 lbs, 5 oz (19.34 lbs)	Lake Casitas, California	Bill Griffith	March 9, 1999
17.	19 lbs, 4 oz (19.25 lbs)	Lake Mira Mesa, California	Chris Brandt	March 22, 1998
18.	19 lbs, 3 oz (19.19 lbs)	Lake Morena, California	Arden Hanline	February 17, 1987
18.	19 lbs, 3 oz (19.19 lbs)	Lake Wohlford, California	Steve Beasley	February 3, 1986
20.	19 lbs, 1/2 ounce (19.06 lbs)**	Lake Miramar, California	Sandy DeFresco	March 14, 1988
20.	19 lbs, 1/2 ounce (19.04 lbs)	Lake Castaic, California	Dan Kadota	January 8, 1989
20.	19 lbs, 1/2 ounce (19.03 lbs)	Success Lake, California	Larry Kerns	January 27, 2001
23.	19 lbs, 0 oz (19.0 lbs)	Lake Tarpon, Florida	Riley Witt	June 21, 1961
24.	18 lbs, 15 oz (18.94 lbs)	Lake Isabella, California	Keith Harper	April, 1984
25.	18 lbs, 14 oz (18.86 lbs)	Lake Castaic, California	Dan Kadota	February 12, 1988
26.	18 lbs, 13 oz (18.81 lbs)	Lake Isabella, California	Joe Weaver	February, 1984
26.	18 lbs, 13 oz (18.81 lbs)	St. Johns River, Florida	Buddy Wright	April 12, 1987
28.	18 lbs, 12 oz (18.75 lbs)	Lake Otay, California	Bob Eberly	March 9, 1980
28.	18 lbs, 12 oz (18.75 lbs)	San Vicente Lake, California	James Steurgeon	March 1, 1981
28.	18 lbs, 12 oz (18.75 lbs)	Lake Castaic, California	Manny Arujo	January 25, 1991
28.	18 lbs, 12 oz (18.75 lbs)	Lake Casitas, California	Marlin Spencer	March 1, 1992

Sources: International Game Fish Association; National Fresh Water Fishing Hall of Fame; Jim Brown of the City of San Diego Lakes; California Department of Fish and Game; the Florida Game and Fresh Water Fish Commission; Western Outdoor News; Bass Anglers Sportsman Society.

*Highly publicized catch was originally submitted at 21 lbs, 10 oz. But during examination, a diving weight of 1 pound 9½ ounces was found inside the fish's stomach.

THE ULTIMATE BASSING TRIP

Bill Rice

Roger Bullock, of Eugene, Oregon, likes to travel economically, and here are his recommendations for a year-long cycle of moving from one prime largemouth location to another.

January—Early prespawn fish, moving from Toledo Bend (TX-LA) to Sam Rayburn (TX), to Lake Okeechobee (FL), then north to Lake Istokpoga and Lake Jackson (FL). On to Camp Hammock on Lake Kissimmee.

February—Caddo Lake (LA-TX), Richland-Chambers Reservoir, Lake Cooper, Lake Fork (TX). East again to Caney Lake (LA) for the excellent postspawn bite, then up the Mississippi Delta. East to Ross Barnett (MS) and Miller's Ferry Reservoir (AL). Dip down to Lake Amistad or Falcon on the Texas-Mexico border.

March-April—Moving northeast, Lake Guntersville (AL), Lake Murray and Santee-Cooper(SC), E. B. Jordan (NC), then west to California's small lunker factories, or to Canyon Lake and Lake Saguaro (AZ) (pray for rain).

April-May—Buggs Island Lake (VA-NC).

June—Lake Champlain (NY-VT-PQ).

July—West to Rice Lake (ON), Lake Minnetonka, Lake Waconia, Pelican Lake (MN). Farther west to Nelson Lake (ND), and south to La Cygne Reservoir (KS).

August, September—Cal Delta, Lake Casitas (CA).

October-November—Back east and south to Lake Guntersville (AL), Lake Seminole (GA).

December—Florida.

NORTHEAST REGION

Lake Champlain (NY-VT-PQ [Quebec]). "Simply the best largemouth fishery in the nation, on top of being my favorite smallmouth destination," says Texas pro Alton Jones. Champlain is a 125-mile-long, 270,000-acre natural lake on the New York-Vermont-Quebec border. Jones claims that from the opener in mid-June to the coldest days of fall, you won't find a slow period: "When I was prefishing there with my son, we caught 20 largemouths in 20 casts—all from 3 to 4 pounds." And that's not to mention the vast schools of smallmouths over 3 pounds and other excellent opportunities. Champlain has a 5-bass daily limit and 10-inch minimum length. Important cover includes weedlines of milfoil, cabbage, lily pads, bulrushes, and water chestnut, as well as boulders and rock points. *Maps:* Fishing Hot Spots, 800/ALL-MAPS. *Contact:* Lake Champlain Chamber of Commerce, 802/863-3489; Plattsburgh-North Country Chamber of Commerce, 518/563-1000; Vermont Fish & Wildlife Department, 802/241-3700; New York Department of Environmental Conservation, 518/457-5420; Quebec Tourism, 800/363-7777. *Guides:* Dave Derner, 802/893-1386; Doug Bishop, 802/287-4092.

Quabbin Reservoir (MA). Much of this quiet, 25,000-acre impoundment scarcely gets fished, thanks to limited access and horsepower restrictions. A top spot for many species, Quabbin can produce 7- to 8-pound largemouths, which move into bays in April and May. No closed season. *Contact:* Metropolitan district Commission Visitors' Center, 413/323-7221.

Connecticut River (VT-NH-MA-CT). This lengthy river offers an angling treat, with big largemouths from its tidal sections north, along with top smallmouth fishing. Look for shoreline wood, weedy backwaters, and tributary creeks. Bonus smallmouths, too. *Contact:* Dave Roberts, 413/665-7636.

Other top options include Lakes Arrowhead and Cobbosseecontee in Maine and New York's Finger Lakes and Oneida Lake.

MID-ATLANTIC REGION

Potomac and James Rivers (MD-VA). Largemouths in the tidal sections here generally run 2 to 4 pounds, with occasional lunkers over 7 pounds. The keys to locating bass in the Potomac are weeds, wood, and tides. Invasions of milfoil and hydrilla have improved bass habitat. Woodcover—old piers, stumps, and fallen trees—hold big fish, particularly when tides are ebbing or flowing. No closed season in tidal Potomac; nontidal waters of MD are catch-and-release only from March 1 through June 15. Minimum-length limit of 15 inches on tidal waters during this period. *Maps:* George Martin, GMCO, 888/420-6277. *Contact:* Washington Visitors and Convention Bureau, 202/293-1958; Charles County Tourism, 800/766-3386; Maryland Department of Natural Resources, Tidewater Administration, 410/974-3061; Virginia Department of Game and Inland Fisheries, 804/367-0509; Susquehana Fishing Tackle, 717/397-1399; *Guide:* Steve Chaconas, 703/360-3472.

Maryland-Virginia inland reservoirs (MD-VA). Tridelphia, Little Seneca, Piney Run, and Rocky Gorge offer 6-pound largemouths to DC-area anglers. Bass get even bigger as you move south: Virginia's Briery Creek reservoir offers likely locations for hooking a 10-pounder. Kerr Reservoir (Buggs Island), on the Virginia-North Carolina border, offers a premier destination for largemouth hunters—one of the best spring locations anywhere. *Contact:* Jim Abers, 804/372-3557; Satterwhite Marina, 252/438-4441.

Kentucky Barkley Lakes (KY). Barkley and adjoining Kentucky Lake continue to be good producers of large bass. Spring action typically begins once water warms into the low 50°F range on secondary points and timbered areas. Check sonar for manmade brushpiles. Spawning occurs near brushy cover. Fish continue to use wood cover in summer, and offshore ledges also hold fish. *Contact:* Lake Barkley State Resort Park, 800/325-1708; Kentucky's Western Wonderland, 800/448-1069; *kentuckylake.com.*

Brett Richardson

Small eastern reservoirs are overlooked sactuaries for big bass.

SOUTHEAST REGION

Lake E. B. Jordan (NC). This impoundment surged onto the big-bass scene in 1994, when lunkers from 8 to over 12 pounds suddenly came on the bite. Big fish begin staging outside the mouths of creeks in March. During summer, fish take to cover including timber, flooded roadbeds, and brushpiles. *Contact:* Mike Dinterman, 919/542-0194.

Falls of The Neuse (NC). Between Raleigh, Durham and Chapel Hill, this 13,000-acre lake produces up to 10-pound bass. Best November-December and February-March. *Contact:* The Tackle Shop, 919/598-1549. *Guides:* Kennon Growe, 919/596-0111; Ed Hancock, 919/562-9110.

Santee-Cooper (SC). This pair of diverse and productive waters has been shining for big bass lately. Search cypress trees, hydrilla beds, humps and channel edges that adorn its 160,000 combined acres. *Contact:* Santee Cooper Country, 800/227-8510.

Lake Murray (SC). This 50,000-acre impoundment on the Saluda River has been a largemouth Mecca since Texas pro Dave Wharton set a tournament-weight record there in 1993. Murray's popularity stems in part from its awesome shallow bite, which can extend for nine months of the year. Its deep basin and diverse habitats seem to keep it more productive than other coastal reservoirs. Important cover includes Brazilian elodea. Prespawn fishing is excellent. *Maps:* Kingfisher Maps, 800/326-0257; Fishing Hot Spots, 800/ALL-MAPS. *Contact:* Dreher Island State Park, 803/364-4152; Greater Columbia Chamber of Commerce, 803/733-1110; Lake Murray Tourism & Recreation, 800/951-4008; South Carolina Department of Natural Resources, 803/734-3889.

The Prespawn Period is prime time for reservoir giants.

Savannah River Chain (SC). These linked reservoirs on the Georgia-South Carolina border are stellar lunker factories, and they just keep improving. Hartwell, Richard B. Russell, and Clark's Hill grow big largemouths. *Contact:* Tracy Watkins, 864/847-7723.

Miller's Ferry Reservoir (AL). This 22,000-acre impoundment is a sleeper for largemouths in the 6- to 9-pound range. Nutrient-rich Alabama River is responsible for size. Hydrilla and other underwater vegetation offer bass plenty of cover. *Contact:* Wilcox County Development Council, 334/682-4929; Roland Cooper State Park, 334/682-4838; Dallas County Chamber of Commerce, 334/875-7241.

Lake Guntersville (AL). This Tennessee River impoundment returns to the top of the charts after a long absence. After a recent visit, Kevin VanDam proclaimed it "the top largemouth lake in the country."

Action starts in February as fish move from deep channels to feeder creeks and the edges of main-lake flats. Carolina rigs take deeper fish, with crankbaits, jerkbaits, and spinnerbaits working on outside grass edges. The vegetation has cleared the reservoir, and big spawning fish can be spotted in creeks and main-lake coves.

During summer, flipping plastics and heavy jigs into grass is productive, along with topwater fishing early in the day. Carolina rigging and drop-shot fishing work on deep structure, creek channel ledges, and along deep grass edges. *Contact:* Goosepond Tackle, 256/574-1083; Scottsboro Chamber of Commerce, 256/259-5500. *Guide:* Troy Jens, 256/534-8657.

FLORIDA

West Lake Tohopekaliga (FL). Known as "Toho," this central Florida lake of 18,810 acres ranks among Bill Dance's all-time favorites, particularly during a new moon in February or March. "Toho offers the best chance of hitting a hot bite from 4- and 5-pound bass, with an 11- or 12-pounder always possible under the next patch of grass," says Dance. "This system's been on an upward spiral since '94. From Toho, you also have access to other lakes on the Kissimmee Chain, notably Lake Kissimmee [35,000 acres], which is in the same class as Toho. A bass close to 15 pounds was taken in Kissimmee not long ago, and the number

Shiner fishing produces personal-best bass for hundreds of visiting anglers every year.

of 10-pounders is rising. The bite's always shallow here." Fourteen-inch minimum length with only one bass 22 inches or over. Important cover —hydrilla and peppergrass beds, emergent vegetation including cutgrass, smartweed, bulrushes, and water hyacinths. Lake scraping slowed the bite in 2005, but it should be storming back. *Maps:* Kingfisher Maps, 800/326-0257; Fishing Hot Spots, 800/ALL-MAPS. *Contact:* Kissimmee Chamber of Commerce, 407/847-3174; Florida Fish and Wildlife Conservation Commission, 352/732-1225; Big Toho Marina, 407/846-2124. *Guides:* Freelancer Guide Service, 800/738-8144.

Other Florida hot spots include Lake Istokpoga (Highland County) and Lake Walk-in-Water—also known as Lake Weohyakapka, in Polk County. Both offer trophy-sized fish, and both have new slot limits that encourage the growth of lunkers. *Guides:* Central Florida Guides, 866/357-7248.

Lake Okeechobee (FL). A perennial favorite, Okeechobee's shallow grassy basin was ravaged by the series of hurricanes that smacked Florida in summer 2004. Anglers have encountered a changed environment and high, murky water but also big concentrations of bass in matted grass. Still lots of 6- to 8-pound bass being caught, so time will tell how quickly the "Big O" takes to return to its prime. *Maps:* Southern Guide Maps, 800/227-8209; Kingfisher Maps, 800/326-0257. *Contact:* Clewiston Chamber of Commerce, 941/983-7979; Okeechobee Chamber of Commerce, 941/763-6464. *Guides:* Chet Douthit, 863/902-9471; Chuck Pippin, 941/564-4273; Roland Martin Marina, 941/983-3151.

Farm 13—Stick Marsh Complex (FL). When good farmland was flooded in the St. Johns River watershed to create this reservoir system, big bass factories were born. *Guides:* Imagination Bassin Guide Services, 772/370-1606; Hugh Crumpler, 321/722-3134.

Istokpoga and Weohyakapka (FL). These two trophy gems are located in central Florida, the former halfway between lakes Kissimmee and Okeechobee, and the latter about 40 miles southeast of Lakeland. Both are managed with 15- to 24-inch protected slot limits, with one trophy over 24 inches permitted and replica mounts of graphite or fiberglass recommended. A drawdown of 28,000-acre Istokpoga in 2001 spurred growth by eliminating excessive shallow muck and thinning hydrilla beds. A 16-pounder was taken in 1998.

Weohyakapka covers 8,000 acres of prime habitat. At peak times, 10-pounders are a daily occurrence. *Contact:* Carroll Hagood, 941/967-8097; Capt. Gene Holbrook, 863/638-2393; Polk County Sports Marketing, 941/534-4370; *cfdc.com.*

TEXAS

Toledo Bend (LA-TX). This 185,000-acre impoundment on the Sabine River has escaped the epidemics that hurt bass populations on reservoirs like Lake Fork and Sam Rayburn. It produces lots of 3- to 6-pounders as well as lunkers up to 15 pounds. Texas pro Jay Yelas recommends February or March prespawn fishing, though there's good fishing at Toledo all year round. No closed season; 8 bass per day limit; minimum length, 14 inches. *Maps:* A.I.D. Associates, 800/AID-MAPS; Fishing Hot Spots, 800/ALL-MAPS; Kingfisher Maps, 800/326-0257. *Contact:* Texas Parks and Wildlife, *tpwd.state.tx.us.* Hemphill Chamber of Commerce, 409/787-2732; Pendleton Harbor Marina, 409/625-4912. *Guides:* Bill Fondren, 409/698-3491; Stephen Johnston, 409/579-4213.

Sam Rayburn (TX). This gigantic East Texas reservoir (114,000 acres) is back with a recent lake record of over 16 pounds. There's no bad time to fish it. When fishing pressure decreases in December and January, lunkers bite in creek channels, over roadbeds, even in dwindling weededges of hydrilla. *Maps:* A.I.D. Associates, 800/AID-MAPS; Fishing Hot Spots, 800/ALL-MAPS. *Contact:* Lufkin Chamber of Commerce, 409/634-6644. *Guides:* Will Kirkpatrick, 409/584-3177; Bill Fondren, 409/698-3491; Stephen Johnston, 409/579-4213.

Lake Fork (TX). Lake Fork (27,500 acres) produces more largemouths for the ShareLunker Program (fish weighing a minimum of 13 pounds) than any other reservoir. Its bass average 4 to 6 pounds, and you've got a good shot at a 10-pounder, particularly in spring and fall. Five-bass daily limit; 14- to 23-inch protected slot limit; only one bass over 23 inches. Important cover includes standing and submerged timber, hydrilla, and submerged roadbeds and ponds. *Maps:* Martin's Maps, 903/297-8780; A.I.D. Associates, 800/AID-MAPS; Fishing Hot Spots, 800/ALL-MAPS. *Contact:* Quitman Chamber of Commerce,903/763-4411; Minnow Bucket Marina, 903/878-2500; Rainswood Marina, 903/473-2494. *Guides:* Dean Stroman, 903/383-7214; Hollice Joiner, 903/878-2500; Dennis Canada, 903/473-8739; Jeff Gunn, 903/765-2155; Richard McCarty, 903/765-2964.

Texas Parks & Wildlife Dept.

Anglers flock to Lake Fork to catch one of its famous lunkers.

Fayette County Reservoir (TX). This relatively small (2,500 acres) bassing playground includes a warmwater discharge, dense hydrilla beds, emergent vegetation (cattails, tules), and timber. Lunkers can be caught even in summer in the warmwater discharge. Slot limits protect the reservoir's abundant 4- to 7-pounders and offer the potential for connecting with giants. Five bass per day limit, with protected slot limit of 14 to 24 inches; only one bass over 24 inches. Important cover includes hydrilla edges, standing timber, creek channels, and emergent vegetation. *Maps:* A.I.D. Associates, 800/AID-MAPS. *Contact:* Fayetteville Chamber of Commerce, 409/378-4021.

Amistad and Falcon (TX-Mexico). The two large gems on the Rio Grande in South Texas have been coming on strong, thanks to greater flows. Their clear waters contain rocky bluffs, offshore points and bars, deep hydrilla walls, sunken brush, and grand bass. Tournament catches over 30 pounds per day are common. *Contact:* Amistad Outdoors, 830/775-0892; Ray Hanselman, 830/774-1857; Falcon Lake Tackle, 956/765-4866, *falconlaketackle.com*; Larry Bridgeman, 956/765-4866.

CENTRAL REGION

Grand Lake (OK). One of the Central Region's most consistent bass producers, this large reservoir offers up many largemouths in the 4- to 5-pound class as well as some lunkers over 8 pounds. It offers excellent fall and winter action on the lower end of the reservoir. Important cover includes ledges, fallen trees, brushpiles, and boat docks. *Contact:* Grand Lakes Association, 918/256-5545.

Other Oklahoma waters. Although Oklahoma largemouths don't grow as large as their Florida-strain cousins to the south in Texas, the Sooner State's bass fisheries are booming, too. Broken Bow has produced a recent state record; Sardis and McGee Creek offer equally fine angling. The largemouths of Lake Watonga, northwest of Oklahoma City, feed on trout and grow to great size, while Sportsman Lake, east of Seminole, also produces lunkers, thanks to its new-lake fertility. Reservoirs like Fort Gibson and Lake Hudson are worth investigating, as well. *Contact:* Oklahoma Department of Wildlife Conservation/Fisheries Div., 405/521-3721; *Guides:* Glen's Guide Service, Broken Bow, 580/494-6047; Guide Chuck Justice, Sardis, McGee Greek, 580/889-6742; Guide James "Doc" Geiger, Fort Gibson, 918/665-0343.

Lake of The Ozarks (MO). This Ozark beauty of 58,000 acres is the favorite largemouth destination of veteran bass pro and former fishery biologist Ken Cook. The reservoir is known for its excellent coldwater bite from December through February, though Cook's favorite season is fall, when largemouths may move into the shallows on main-lake points to attack passing schools of shad. Six-bass daily limit; 15-inch minimum. Important cover includes boat docks, submerged stumps and timber, fallen trees, rock bluffs and points. *Maps:* Fishing Hot Spots, 800/ALL-MAPS. *Contact:* Lake of The Ozarks Convention & Visitors Bureau, 800/FUN-LAKE; Missouri Dept. of Conservation, 573/751-4115; *Guide:* L. D. Wimbs, 800/348-5214.

Truman Lake (MO). This large (55,600 acres), complex reservoir gives bass plenty of room to roam. Spring fishing is predictably good. Largemouths grow fast in Truman's dark, fertile waters. Important cover includes standing timber. Minimum-length limit of 15 inches. *Contact:* Truman Lake Regional Association, 800/299-0015; Bucksaw Point Marina, 816/477-3323.

La Cygne Reservoir (KS). This is the likeliest water north of Oklahoma for a 10-pounder in the Central Region. The reservoir receives warm water from a power plant, which means that bass get a longer growing season than they receive in other reservoirs or farm ponds, reducing overwintering mortality and increasing forage. That combination of advantages produces the only true lunkers in the region. Western Kansas reservoirs worth fishing are Cedar Bluff, Sebelius, Webster, and Kirwin, whose current fecundity is like that of new lakes. The state has purchased irrigation rights to these reservoirs, ensuring that their water levels remain stable. *Contact:* Kansas Travel, 800/2KANSAS.

NORTH-CENTRAL REGION

Lake Minnetonka (MN). Just west of the Twin Cities, Minnetonka is a boat-heavy, 14,500-acre lake whose average 4- to 5-pound largemouths rival bass fishing anywhere in the country. Minnetonka's 16 individual basins, connected by channels, create over 100 miles of shoreline and a wide variety of habitat and water conditions. During early season, its shallow bays hold large numbers of spawning and postspawn bass. Important cover includes docks, rocks, and beds of milfoil. Closed season from mid-February until Saturday of Memorial Day weekend; 6-fish daily bag limit; no minimum length. In Minnesota: Scores of other excellent lakes, with top-end size around 6 pounds. *Maps:* Fishing Hot Spots, 800/ALL-MAPS; LakeMaster, 320/632-6300. *Contact:* Minnesota Office of Tourism, 800/657-3700; Minnesota Department of Natural Resources, 651/296-3325.

Other top Minnesota lakes include Waconia, Minnewaska, Pokegama, Pelican (Orr), and Prior.

Nelson Lake (ND). This impoundment remains North Dakota's top trophy bass water, producing many fish over 5 pounds. With incoming warm water from a power plant and fertilized water from nearby farms, Nelson offers better forage and a longer growing season than other waters in the state. *Contact:* North Dakota State Game and Fish Department, 701/328-6300.

Shabbona, LaSalle, Rend, Carlyle, and Shelbyville reservoirs (IL). The best largemouth fishing in years is possible on these Illinois reservoirs, thanks to stocking and strict harvest limits. LaSalle, a cooling reservoir opened to fishing in 1987, now offers the possibility of connecting with 7- to 8-pounders. Lake Bloomington is a smaller gem in that city. *Contact:* Illinois Department of Natural Resources, *dnr.state.il.us.* *Guide:* Jim Crowley, 309/827-2103.

Lake Monroe (IN). This reservoir offers the best Indiana shot at a giant, with plenty of 6- to 7-pounders and occasional fish over 10. *Contact:* Bloomington Convention & Visitors Bureau, 812/334-8900. *Guide:* Chris Walker, 317/727-8432.

Eastern South Dakota boasts several small lakes that offer excellent bass fishing . In **Iowa**, small public impoundments offer a shot at a 7-pounder. West Okoboji also offers excellent largemouth and smallmouth fishing.

The North-central region boasts abundant natural lakes and small impoundments with superb bass fishing.

FAR WEST

Cal Delta (CA). The Sacramento-San Joaquin Delta is a complex river system of over 2,000 square miles. It contains old river channels, sloughs, oxbows, and manmade ship channels—all of which hold fish. Three- to 6-pounders are common, with potential for 10-pound catches. The spring (February through mid-April) prespawn bite is superior. River and tidal currents—the Delta empties into the northeastern end of San Francisco Bay—keep the system dynamic even in blistering-hot summers. Increased habitat for bass in the form of hydrilla, milfoil, coontail, lily pads, and water hyacinths have turned this into a largemouth Mecca. Five-fish daily limit, 12-inch minimum length limit. *Maps:* Fish-N-Map Co., 303/421-5994. *Contact:* Stockton Chamber of Commerce, 209/547-2770; Antioch Chamber of Commerce, 510/757-1800; Outdoor Sportsman, 209/957-4867. *Guides:* Andy Cuccia, 925/625-5148; Bobby Barrack, 925/684-9904.

Lake Casitas (CA). Located 80 miles north of Los Angeles, this 2,000-acre impoundment is legendary for its largemouth records. Giants bite best when they move onto shallower structure during the Prespawn Period from late January until April. Stocker rainbow trout bulk up Casitas' largemouths to incredible size—a 25-incher might weigh 15.5 pounds, compared to 9 pounds at Stick Marsh (FL) and 12 at Lake Fork (TX). Important cover includes a large island, extended brushy flats, creek channels, and deep ledges. *Maps:* Fishing Hot Spots, 800/ALL-MAPS; Fish 'n' Map Co., 303/421-5994. *Contact:* Lake Casitas Recreation Area, 805/649-2233; Ojai Chamber of Commerce, 805/646-8126; Ventura Chamber of Commerce, 805/648-2875. *Guide:* Shawn Rogers, 949/586-4308.

Lake Castaic (CA). Forty miles north of Los Angeles, Castaic is a 2,000-acre reservoir that gained attention in the early 1990s for its huge largemouths, including Bob Crupi's 22.01-pounder. The intense fishing pressure that followed Crupi's catch reduced the water's big bass. Attention has shifted since then away from the main reservoir to Castaic's afterbay, a pool below the reservoir that stripers haven't invaded. *Contact:* Los Angeles Dept. of Parks and Recreation, 661/257-4050. *Guides:* Sean Rogers, 949/422-0869; Troy Folkestad, 949/582-7588.

Clear Lake (CA). California's largest reservoir, this 44,000-acre impoundment 90 miles northeast of San Francisco is currently in a boom cycle, typically producing handsome 3- to 6-pound largemouths. Ten-pounders have become almost common catches for springtime experts and night anglers. Sight-fishing can be phenomenal, although fishing pressure can make lunkers hard to tempt. An excellent topwater bite is available from late spring into early summer. *Maps:* Fishing Hot Spots, 800/ALL-MAPS; Fish 'n' Map Co., 303/421-5994. *Contact:* Clear Lake Chamber of Commerce, 707/994-3600; Clear Lake State Park, 707/279-4293. *Guides:* Jim Munk, 707/987-3734; Larry Hemphill, 530/674-0276.

Other California Lakes. Lots of small waters produce big bass. *Info:* Western Outdoor News, *wonews.com.*

Pleasant, Bartlett, and Saguaro (AZ). Arizona's big-three reservoirs, though small by Texas standards, produce giant bass, with a few running from 14 to 16 pounds. Habitat improvement by conservation groups and government agencies has been critical to this success. If currently low waters persist, however, Arizona's largemouth fisheries may suffer. *Contact;* Fountain Hills Chamber of Commerce (Lake Saguaro), 480/837-1654.

NORTHWEST REGION

Potholes Reservoir (WA). This 25,000-acre impoundment provides good habitat for largemouths, growing them to a possible 10 pounds. **Lake Washington (WA).** Here's a surprise: Lake Washington—covered with boats, bridged by heavy-duty freeway traffic—is full of largemouths, according to Washington bass expert Jeff Boyer. *Contact:* Washington Department of Fish and Wildlife, *wdfw.wa.gov/contact.htm*, 360/902-2200.

CANADA

Rice Lake (ON). The best big-bass factory north of the U.S.-Canadian border, this 18-mile-long, 22,000-acre lake is part of the Trent-Severn Waterway, which includes the Kawartha Chain of Lakes, spanning 240 miles of southern Ontario northwest of Peterborough. Cover includes bulrushes and weedy flats over clear water. *Guides:* Rocky Crawford, 905/430-9039; Don Faster, 800/489-7885.

Lake Simcoe (ON). Better known for its smallmouth fishing, this lake just north of Toronto is also a largemouth prize. Cabbage and coontail as deep as 20 feet provide excellent habitat in massive Cooks Bay. *Contact:* Ontario Travel Centre, 800/567-1140.

Bay of Quinte (ON-PQ). On the north shore of Lake Ontario between Toronto and Quebec lies Quinte, home to some of the biggest walleyes in North America, but it will soon be famous for its largemouth bass, as well. Clearing water has promoted the expansion of lush aquatic weeds. Cover: weeds, fallen trees, boat docks. *Contact:* Ontario Ministry of Natural Resources, *mnr.gov.on.ca/MNR/fishing/*, 800/667-1940. Other top prospects include Tri-Lakes (Chemong, Pigeon, Buckhorn), Big Rideau, Lake Couchiching, and Lake Scugog in Ontario and Lac St. Louis, Quebec.

Mark Krupa

Canadian lakes contain lots of surprisingly big largemouth bass.

Pigeon, Buckhorn, and Chemung lakes (ON). Like Rice, the interconnected Tri-Lakes are part of the Kawartha chain. At 12,000 acres, Pigeon is the largest. The northern portion, around the resort town of Bobcaygeon, is deeper and rockier than the southern half around Emily Provincial Park. Buckhorn Lake (7,000 acres), which lies to the east of Pigeon, offers everything from slop fields to deep rockpiles, island points, and boat docks. Chemung Lake (5,000 acres) is known for its weedgrowth, especially south of the causeway at Bridgenorth.

Guide: Rocky Crawford, 905/430-9039. *Accommodations and information:* MNR, Peterborough District, 705/755-2000; Bobcaygeon Chamber of Commerce, 705/738-2202; Ontario Travel Information Center, Central Region, 705/725-7280; Get Away Country Travel, 800/461-1912.

Lake Couchiching (ON). Plenty of bass from 3 to 5 pounds for anglers who pick jigs through coontail and hydrilla beds. Or concentrate on any of the weededges bordering the deep clear basin.

Contact: Backwater Tackle Shop, 800/675-4071; MNR, Midhurst District, 705/725-7523; Huronia/Lakelands Travel Association, 800/487-6642; Ontario Travel Information Center, Central Region, 705/725-7280.

Big Rideau Lake (ON). A deep, clear-water gem 50 miles southwest of Ottawa. Schools of bass work classic weed structure but also sometimes roam open water.

Contact: Eastern Ontario Travel Association, 800/567-3278; Get Away Country Travel, 800/461-1912; Patrick Curran, Ontario East Tourism, 800/567-3278.

Weslemkoon, Limerick, Lingham, and Wollaston lakes (ON). These waters have for years produced largemouth bass in the 5- to 7-pound range. Also explore some of the tiny lakes and potholes scattered throughout the rolling hardwood countryside.

Contact: Eastern Ontario Travel Association, 800/567-3278; Patrick Curran, Ontario East Tourism, 800/567-3278; Bancroft & District Chamber of Commerce, 613/332-1513.

Long Point Bay (ON). 170,000 acres on Lake Erie. The best fishing is in the shallow weed, reed, and lily pad riddled Inner Bay, near the town of Port Rowan and Long Point Provincial Park, and in the backwaters encircled by Pottohawk Point and Ryersons Island.

Contact: Ontario Travel Centre, Niagara/Southwestern Region, 905/871-3505; Sandra Chabot, Southwestern Ontario Travel Association, 800/661-6804; Peter McFadden, Festival County Travel, 800/267-3399. Guide: Greg Horoky, 519/738-3095.

MEXICO

Mexico's reservoirs produce lots of extraordinarily large bass—it's easy to imagine a world record coming from this country. They're fished only 8 or 9 months, typically from October into June, by comparatively few anglers. Because guide boats are equipped with outboards in the 40- to 60-hp range, and reservoirs range from 20,000 to 90,000 acres, bass sanctuaries abound. Compared to the fishing pressure on reservoirs north of the border at Lake Fork or Sam Rayburn in Texas, or Castaic and Casitas in California, Mexican impoundments see minimal angling pressure, though substantial gillnetting occurs at some locations.

Lake Baccarac (Sinaloa, MX). This older Mexican reservoir (35,000 acres) is worth a trip to anyone looking for a giant largemouth. Hit the prespawn right—it's sometime between late December and mid-February—and you may catch several 10-pounders a day, with others between 3 and 7 pounds. Baccarac has produced two bass over 19 pounds, including the Mexican record of 19-10. *Contact:* Fishing Trips of a Lifetime, 405/354-0358.

El Salto (Mazatlan, MX). This 20,000-acre irrigation reservoir north of Mazatlan, impounded in 1983, holds lots of 10-pounders and numbers of fish to 14. Forage includes shad and tilapia. *Contact:* Hook Sportfishing, 800/583-8133, *hooksportfishing.com*; Ron Speed's Adventures, 903/489-1656; *www.anglersinn.com*.

Lake Comedero. Like El Salto, 27,000-acre Comedero is close to Mazatlan. It was opened to fishing in the mid-1980s and stocked with northern and then Florida strains of bass. Teen-weight bass are taken occasionally during prime time. Its accommodations and surroundings are more rustic, but the lunker hunting is good. *Contact:* Ron Speed Adventures, 903/489-1656.

Lake Huites (Sinaloa, MX). Huites is a high-elevation lake that offers spectacular scenery and outstanding bass action. Catch-rates of over 100 fish per day are common; fish from 7 to over 10 pounds are, too, when water levels are adequate.

A Mexican bass trip makes a fine vacation, with a good shot at a 10-pounder.

Fall and spring offer the best action. *Contact:* Trophy Bass Lodge, 888/769-0220, *bassmex.com*; Lake Huites Lodge, 888/744-8867.

Aqua Milpa (Nayarit, MX). This huge (60-mile-long) reservoir is located near Tepic in the state of Nayarit. Expect lots of 3- to 7-pound bass, though its fast-growing bass have reached 10 pounds in only five years because of abundant threadfin shad, a more constant water level, and more stable climate than other Mexican impoundments offer. *Contact:* Hook Sportfishing, 800/583-8133; Fishing Trips of A Lifetime, 405/354-0358.

Lake Guerrero (Tamaulipas, MX). Guerrero was impounded in 1971, the big (90,000-plus acres) reservoir that put Mexican bass on the map. Its fluctuating water levels have proven harmful to consistent production of lunkers, but giants up to 14 pounds continue to be caught there. *Contact:* Fishing Trips of A Lifetime, 405/354-0358.

El Cuchillo (Monterrey, MX). Newest of Mexico's bass lakes. El Cuchillo in the state of Nuevo Leon offers classic brush and creek channel habitat. Located in a state park, netting is forbidden. *Contact:* Best For Bass, best_for_bass@hotmail.com; Guide Carlos Gloria, crgloria@yahoo.com.

FUTURE PROSPECTS FOR GIANT BASS

Florida bass have changed the history of bass fishing in the West and South. Anglers can expect to boat 10-pounders in these warmwater parts of the country, and those who return home to chillier regions have frequently put pressure on their state and provincial governments to stock Florida-strain fish in local waters. Once electrophoresis made typing an individual fish's genetic makeup possible, it became clear that Florida bass were unsuited to northern climes. Studies have demonstrated that in marginally warm waters—even some places in Texas—Florida-strain fish do less well than native or previously stocked northern strains. Some Texas waters are simply too marginal in terms of year-round temperature to sustain pure Florida strains of fish. In northern Oklahoma, where winters can often be severe, Florida-strain bass can't sustain their numbers.

The story is different in warmwater Texas, Arizona, and California, where Florida-strain bass have transformed bass fishing. Eleven of the 20 largest bass ever recorded in Texas had some Florida genes. Pure Florida-strain bass in Texas's Lake Aquilla, a study at Texas A & M University revealed, grew faster than hybrids or northern-strain largemouths. Hybrids between the two strains were intermediate in growth and spawning time.

Farther west, the success of Florida-strain largemouths is more emphatic. Orville Ball, former lake superintendent for the City of San Diego, recalls that before that city's reservoirs were planted with Florida bass in 1959, "A 9-pounder was the largest largemouth anyone ever caught. If you caught a 6-pounder, you were a hero." By 1973, the state record had climbed from 14 to almost 21 pounds. Anglers here built reputations around catching giants, from "Lunker" Bill Murphy in the 1980s to Bob Crupi in the 1990s, and now to today's top lunker hunters like Bill Siemantel, Mike Long, and Jed Dickerson.

California's current position as a lunker largemouth factory has been fueled by several factors: Its receptive climate to lunker-strain bass; its booming population and resulting impoundment-building; voluntary catch and release, and management that encourages the growth of lunkers, particularly the stocking of rainbow trout. Interestingly, southern California largemouth pioneers Murphy and Ball witnessed not only Florida bass changing California's bass fishery, but California also changing Florida bass: "Originally the bass stayed shallow," reported the late Bill Murphy. "They marauded more. Now they've adjusted to their new environment and use deeper water," he observes. "Reservoir levels fluctuate so much that bass don't orient around shallow cover. Instead, they live off-shore or near deep structure. Shifting water levels move prey-fish inshore and offshore and make them more vulnerable. The adaptable bass has adjusted to such habitat. It's one of the things that makes California giant-bass fisheries unlike any others."

If you work to improve water quality, forage, and cover on your home waters, you'll have the satisfaction of knowing your local largemouths are as good and as vigourous as any on the planet.

Can California and Mexican bass fisheries, the most notable in recent decades for size and vigor, grow bigger fish?

Judging from existing records in these locations, as well as from other state and national records, it would seem that natural limits have been reached—if new records are set, they'll probably differ only by a few ounces. Old records suggest why this is the case: As an example, the biggest northern largemouth ever recorded is a 15½-pounder caught through the ice in Massachusetts in 1975. George Perry's longstanding 22-lb. 4-oz. Georgia record, according to Dr. David Philipp, the premier bass geneticist in the U.S., was probably a natural intergrade between a northern and a Florida-strain bass. The current California record, a 22-lb. Florida-strain bass caught by Bob Crupi in 1991, may represent maximum size for largemouth bass.

The observations and studies of these and other lunker hunters seem to come down to this: Size is governed by genetics, to a large extent, and strains develop in response to the rigors of life in native waters. Some fishery managers argue that habitat alterations and past fish-stock transfers have so scrambled the natural genetic adaptations of strains and races, that there's not much sense in worrying about trying to conserve genetically distinct strains. Most geneticists advocate conservatism in stock transfers to avoid worsening the present very altered situation.

The quest for giant bass is likely to take you far away from your home waters from time to time, and we wish you well in your search for the ultimate lunker. At the same time, we hope you honor the remarkable strength and adaptability of the largemouths that inhabit your nearby streams, lakes, and reservoirs. If they've been there for more than a few generations, they are native to those places and should be cherished for that reason. They're as big for their own waters as any Mexican lunker bass in its subtropical 25,000-acre reservoir. If you work to improve existing water quality, forage, and cover on your homewaters, you'll have the considerable satisfaction of knowing that your local largemouths are as healthy and vigorous as any on the planet. Maybe not the biggest, but among the best.

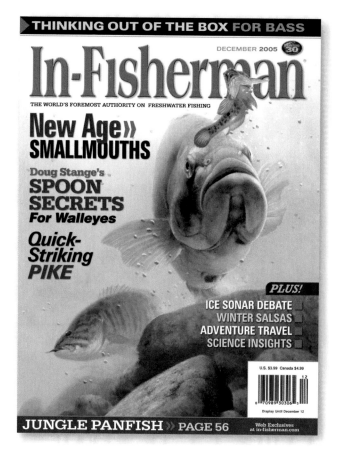

Visit The Top Fishing
Destination In The World

TIPS FROM THE EXPERTS

In-Fisherman pros provide tips and advice to help you catch more fish.

IN-FISHERMAN MERCHANDISE

Great deals on Award-Winning books, videos, and more.

BEST FISHING TIMES

Plan to be on the water when the bite is hot.

BIG FISH GALLERY

Show off your catch and see what our readers are catching.

FISH ID

Not sure what you just caught? Look it up here.

in-fisherman.com

ASK THE DOCS

Our experts answer your electronics and motor questions.

RECIPES

Fish are nutritious and delicious—especially when prepared from an In-Fisherman recipe.

PROFESSIONAL WALLEYE TRAIL

Watch tourney results as they happen or sign up with a pro!

IN-FISHERMAN TV & RADIO

See what's on tap this week for IF TV and locate the IF Radio station in your area.

In-Fisherman
TEACHING THE WORLD HOW TO FISH!
ON THE INTERNET

7819 Highland Scenic Rd, Baxter, MN 56425